"Collections of reflections by serious spiritual guides such as Ted Dunn are a gift to us all." **Joan Chittister, OSB. Former President of LCWR and the Benedictine Federation, internationally renowned author and lecturer, Erie, PA**

"Religious have long embraced the notion of Transformation as an invitation into the graced empowerment of God, but as Ted Dunn reminds us, it can be ". . . downright messy and painful. Transformation is inherently complex, conflictual, intimate, ambiguous, and risky - and the results are always unpredictable." Yet this is a book offering strategies and guidelines that are essentially hopeful and empowering.

Religious Congregations that have worked with Ted Dunn are all too familiar with his forthright sense of challenge: "When a community has more memories than dreams, it is dying." At the graced crossroads of Religious Life today, dreaming our way ahead, even through the portals of decline and diminution, is the greatest challenge facing us all. To do that all important work with honesty, imagination, and integrity is Ted Dunn's aspiration in the work of transformation, for which this book will be an invaluable resource." **Diarmuid O'Murchu, M.S.C. Social psychologist, internationally renowned author and lecturer, Dublin, Ireland**

"In this companion book to author's inspiring, *Graced crossroads: pathways to deep change and transformation,* Ted Dunn invites both individuals, faith organizations, and religious congregations to the deep and soulful work of transformation. He artfully and tenderly leads the reader into the inner terrain of our being where the Spirit's work of integration and transformation abounds. By utilizing his decades of experience with religious congregations, Ted Dunn garners the wisdom found when individuals and committed teams walk the sacred journey of transformation amidst the gritty realities found at the crossroads of life." **Jayne Helmlinger, CSJ. Former President of LCWR and General Superior of the Sisters of St. Joseph of Orange, CA**

"Dr. Ted's invitation to go deeper into the process of transformation was embraced by our monastic community. The result was a deeper healing of relationships, thus drawing us closer together as a community. There exists a new gentleness and peace among us. We are so grateful!" **Terri Hoffman, OSB. Prioress, Mother of God Monastery, Watertown, SD**

"In *The Inner Work of Transformation*, Ted Dunn invites both individuals and communities into the soulwork of transformation. These poignant reflections and thought-provoking questions have challenged me on my own journey, to accept God's invitation to go deeper and to embrace each next step toward wholeness and freedom. The five dynamic elements of transformation which Ted identifies—shifts in consciousness, reclaiming your inner voice, reconciliation and conversion, experimentation and learning, and transformative visioning—continue to serve as guideposts in my life, for we are all lifelong learners who are united in our vulnerability. This book has also been a rich source of communal transformation in the Tiffin Franciscan community, as we utilized these reflections in small groups with meaningful sharing. As one newer to Religious Life, professing perpetual vows four years ago, I find great hope in Ted's writing and believe it to be a source of encouragement for any individual or community who takes seriously the call to transformation."
Marcia Boes, OSF. Sisters of St. Francis of Tiffin, OH

THE
INNER WORK
OF
Transformation

A GUIDE FOR PERSONAL REFLECTION

AND COMMUNAL SHARING

TED DUNN

THE

INNER WORK

OF

Transformation

A GUIDE FOR PERSONAL REFLECTION

AND COMMUNAL SHARING

THE

INNER WORK

OF

Transformation

A GUIDE FOR PERSONAL REFLECTION

AND COMMUNAL SHARING

Ted Dunn

CCS Publications

www.CCSstlouis.com

Published in the United States by CCS Publications, Comprehensive Consulting Services, Clearwater, Florida: www.CCSstlouis.com

Permissions

Unless otherwise stated, Dr. Ted Dunn uses his own translation and/or paraphrase of Scripture. Dr. Dunn draws from a variety of sources, especially the New International Version and the New Living Translation. His practice is to reference chapter and verse for scriptural sources, but not to identify precise translations.

Library of Congress Cataloging-in-Publication Data

Dunn, Ted

The inner work of transformation : a guide for personal reflection and communal sharing / Ted Dunn

ISBN: 978-1-09839-404-2

ebook ISBN: 978-1-09839-405-9

Printed in the United States of America

First Edition

To all those faith communities who are facing a crossroads and are ardently hoping to transform their lives and give birth to new life.

ACKNOWLEDGEMENTS

This guide for the inner work of transformation emerged from my ministry accompanying communities through a Journey of Transformation. While there are issues common to all communities who face these times of transition, each one has its unique story as well as its own history, traditions, culture and spirituality to bring to these crossroads. It is never an easy path. It is always filled with both promise and peril. I have had the unique privilege of walking with many who have summoned the courage, creativity and tenacity needed to take such a journey.

I have offered many of the reflections you will find in this book to those communities with whom I have guided through a Journey of Transformation. Each community with whom I have accompanied has gifted me with the opportunity to grow in my own spiritual journey. They have challenged me to grapple with my own faith, doubts and questions about the role of God and grace in my own transformative experiences. These reflections are one way for me to give something of myself that I hope will be received as intended: a gesture of thanks and a stimulus for your own inner work.

I am grateful to all those communities who have allowed me to walk so intimately with them through a Journey of Transformation. I am grateful for the depth and seriousness with which they engaged the kind of material I am now sharing more widely. Your feedback, challenges, support and suggestions over the years have contributed substantially to reflections presented here.

I also want to thank my wife, Beth who helped me live into the same kinds of questions I am inviting you to explore. She has been, and continues to be, my companion in my own Journey of Transformation. I wish to thank Theresa LaMetterey, a Sister of St. Joseph of Orange, who carefully read, studied and edited my manuscript. Her feedback was enormously helpful in elevating the caliber of my own writing.

God speaks to each of us as he makes us,
then walks with us silently out of the night.

These are the words we dimly hear:

You, sent out beyond your recall,
go to the limits of your longing.
Embody me.

Flare up like a flame
and make big shadows I can move in.

Let everything happen to you: beauty and terror.
Just keep going. No feeling is final.
Don't let yourself lose me.

Nearby is the country they call life.
You will know it by its seriousness.

Give me your hand.
Rainer Maria Rilke. Go to the limits of your longing.

CONTENTS

FOREWORD

No matter what kind of life altering scenario plunges a person or community into deep, dark, rock-bottom-painful places, once you come up for air and into the light, there are choices to be made at the crossroads. Our community could have made a choice to do nothing. We could have continued to replay the same old narrative telling ourselves, "That's just the way it is," never stopping to consider why *you* are the way *you* are. Tempting though it was to make that choice to go down that familiar path and repeat the familiar narratives, we chose to forge a new path and create a new narrative for ourselves. We chose to embrace *The Inner Work of Transformation* as a means for claiming a new life.

Our community had come to what Dr. Ted Dunn refers to as a "graced crossroad."[i] It was a painful place for us, a kind of bottom, and the beginning of what Ted calls a Journey of Transformation. Ted, along his wife and partner, Dr. Beth Lipsmeyer, led us forward using processes of deep change. The journey has been a mixture of grieving, gestation, and giving birth. They trained our community to work skillfully through the chaos and wilderness of transformation.[1] We were invited to give voice to our deepest longings. We were encouraged to reconcile our wounds and claim our authentic inner voice.

---

1 A powerful skills training for communities, what Drs. Ted and Beth refer to as Conversational Approach to Relational Effectiveness (CARE)

We were inspired to tap our pioneering spirit, to experiment with new ways of being and to become a learning community.

These processes provided us with a method and a means to grow. We have been inspired to stretch our thinking, walk across new thresholds, and live into new possibilities. We have opened new doors and shaped a future we never could have imagined, and certainly could not have done, if we had only used strategic planning. We have gained a renewed strength and commitment to be-in-it-together and a desire to keep listening for that "deeper invitation." Ted's processes and reflections, shared here in *The Inner Work of Transformation*, have enabled us to listen and respond to the deeper invitation.

It is one thing to do inner work with a counselor or spiritual director and quite another to do this kind of work as a faith community. This kind of soul-work is difficult and demanding, even if done privately with a counselor or spiritual director. It is the kind of work that takes guts and a willingness to be vulnerable. With the processes laid out in this book, a deeper challenge arises: sharing it with the people who live life with you in community.

It took us a little over a year to complete Ted's reflections, exercises and invitations to share with one another. We each took time for personal reflection, then each small group shared the fruits of their inner work. The accomplishment of having done this inner work together strengthened our esteem as a community. Our respect and appreciation for each other soared. Engaging in this inner work together on this Journey of Transformation gave us comfort and unearthed our collective wisdom. It has been the glue that holds us together.

There is a lot to the Journey of Transformation and our story is still being written. It may sound trite, but I believe it to be true: we must perform while we transform. Without a commitment to do the inner work, the deep engagement with each other, and the effort to write a new narrative, our community could have, probably would have, sunk under the weight of it all.

While on this Journey of Transformation, we have brushed up against the mystery of transformation through our own experiences, learning not only what it means to survive but to thrive. Tremendous fruit has been borne out of our transformative labor; so much so, that we are reclaiming our inner voice and listening to our true selves. We are acting our way into a new way of being, shaping a new vision for our future, and creating a life with meaning and purpose. May you and your community find these same kinds of treasures as you engage in *The Inner Work of Transformation*.

Barbara Younger, OSB. Leadership Team, Mother of God Monastery, Watertown, South Dakota.

Preface

Yet the Lord pleads with you still: Ask where the good road is, the godly paths you used to walk in, in the days of long ago. Travel there, and you will find rest for your souls.
Jeremiah 6:16

I offer this guide to the inner work of transformation for individuals and communities who have reached a crossroads in life and are looking for ways to bring forth new life through processes that promote transformation. It represents the kind of soulwork I believe is too often neglected but nonetheless essential to the successful transformation of communities and the individuals who reside in them.

My ministry over the last few decades has been primarily with Catholic religious communities. As a group, they are going through an enormous transition and I have accompanied many of them through what I call a "Journey of Transformation." The foundations for my work on personal and communal transformation was recently published in a book entitled, *Graced crossroads: pathways to deep change and transformation*. I indicated in that foundational publication that this companion book on the inner work of transformation would follow.

This book provides a series of reflections and suggested processes aimed at helping those who wish to do this kind of soulwork. It is meant to be a resource, not some kind of seven-point program for guaranteed transformation. There is no such thing. I do not presume to think that what I am offering is the only way that such inner work can be done. However, it is one way that I have found to be highly effective. The communities whom I have been accompanying, and who have engaged in this inner work, have found it to be integral to their larger Journey of Transformation.

It is written primarily for faith communities and you will find that many of the reflections, poems and quotes I use are Christian. However, I include materials and quotes from a variety of other faiths and people of wisdom. Consequently, I believe that the material is suitable for communities of any faith. In fact, I would believe it is suitable for churches, leadership teams, and non-profit organizations, any group for whom their mission (not money) is the bottom line. It is written for any group that is facing a crossroads and seeking new life through transformative processes. It is for those who recognize that the heart of such efforts is a spiritual journey.

Making this work your own

I know of no other personal work that can be done that is more intimate than the soulwork of our lives. No spiritual director or religious leader can describe for you what is in your own soul or prescribe for you your own spiritual pathway of transformation. Your own name for "God," the "Divine," or the "soul," your own experience of the sacred, and your own understanding of what constitutes a spiritual journey, is for each person to claim. While as a community you have undoubtably claimed a common mission and spirituality, each individual's spiritual journey is unique.

Johann Wolfgang von Goethe once said: "All truly wise thoughts have been thought already thousands of times; but to make them truly ours, we must think them over again honestly, till they take root in our personal experience." The same is true here. *The Inner Work of Transformation* is not something that can be done for you by leadership or outsourced to a committee. The only way this guide will hold meaning for you is if the material I am offering, along with the added meditative touchstones, take root in your own experience. May this guide to your inner work of transformation be an invitation that brings you to wholeness, healing and a greater union with one another and the Divine.

Introduction

Stand still. The trees ahead and bushes beside you
Are not lost. Wherever you are is called Here
And you must treat it as a powerful stranger,
Must ask permission to know it and be known.
The forest breathes. Listen. It answers,
I have made this place around you.
If you leave it, you may come back again, saying Here.
No two trees are the same to Raven.
No two branches are the same to Wren.
If what a tree or a bush does is lost on you,
You are surely lost. Stand still. The forest knows
Where you are. You must let it find you.
David Wagoner. Lost

Context and purpose

The Inner Work of Transformation is a guide for assisting faith communities
and mission driven organizations who have reached some kind of crossroads
and are looking for ways to choose life anew, to transform their lives and give

birth to a new narrative for their lives. I use the term "community" rather broadly for the purpose of this book. My primary focus is on members of a community who are, or hope to be, collectively engaged in communal transformation. In essence, this guide is for all those who want to proactively cooperate with grace by doing the soulwork of deep change and transformation.

All of us can learn to do the work of cooperating with grace in the Divine Mystery of transformation. It is the soulwork we must do when faced with a graced crossroads in life, when there is no going back to the way things were, and when the way forward is uncertain and ambiguous. When this soulwork is done in the context of a faith community, or any team or organization for whom mission is the bottom line, it facilitates their collective transformation.

The Divine Mystery of transformation will forever remain inscrutable and beyond human comprehension. I would not presume to have broken the code. However, there is a great deal of wisdom we can glean if we reflect deeply upon our own transformative life experiences. And there is considerable knowledge we can glean from recent advances in the humanities and science, as well as from contemporary and ancient faith traditions. We can now identify much of what we can do, what constitutes our own inner work of transformation, while the rest is left to mystery and the workings of grace.

We know, for instance, the difference between change and transformation. We know all too well what the well-trodden path of least resistance looks like and its inevitable outcome of decay and death. While we cannot know the precise path or outcomes of a transformative journey, we know what helps us to walk this path and we know what gets in our way. We know the paradox and importance of taking the responsibility to plan our future, while simultaneously recognizing that we cannot predict, control and engineer the mystery of transformation. We know the importance of integrating our plans with the inner work of transformation so as to cooperate with grace in a journey of transformation.

Like the trees and the bushes, we are not lost. The soul knows its way. We have merely to stand still, listen to that still small voice, then do our part in cooperating with grace. The inner work of transformation is the part we can do, what communities can do, to cooperate with grace in their journey of transformation.

Graced crossroads: pathways to deep change and transformation

The Inner Work of Transformation is a companion to the book I recently published to explore the nature of transformation and how to engage in the work of communal transformation. That foundational book entitled, *Graced Crossroads: Pathways to Deep Change and Transformation*, addressed four central questions:

1. What are the graced crossroads religious communities are now facing and the deeper invitations calling them to the inner work of transformation?

2. What are the challenges and opportunities in our world and within Religious Life that have brought communities to these graced crossroads?

3. How might communities assess their capacity to engage in communal transformation, what will it ask of them, and what can they expect to come from it?

4. What does a Journey of Transformation truly involve and how can communities proactively engage in this Divine Mystery?

While the impetus for that work was brought about because of the particular crossroads Catholic religious communities are facing, its foundational principles and guidance are applicable to any community. And, while the focus was on communal transformation, the foundational principles and processes are equally applicable to personal transformation. Because that book was foundational and conceptual, it could not provide the kind of reflections and guidance presented here for the personal and interpersonal work of transformation.

The Inner Work of Transformation picks up where *Graced Crossroads* left off. This book provides 20 reflections to guide those who wish to transform their lives through their own personal and communal soulwork. These reflections will assist individuals in their personal work of transformation and, through the sharing among members of a community, will facilitate their collective efforts toward communal transformation.

Misguided efforts and the alternative

Communal transformation starts within the heart and soul of individuals who make up a community. Transformation is a soul to surface, inward, upward and outward spiraling movement. If the individuals who make up a community are not fully engaged in this kind of soulwork, efforts to bring about communal transformation are doomed to failure. Organizational change might occur in the absence of this kind of inner work, but organizational transformation will not.

Most communities facing a crossroads and expressing a desire to transform and renew their lives end up focusing on organizational change and neglecting the inner work required of communal transformation. They will use conventional approaches, such as strategic planning, to address these organizational changes and avoid the kind of deep change required of individuals to transform the culture and soul of community.

Conventional methods are simply not suited for unconventional times like these. The research indicates that the vast majority of these efforts, upwards of 80%, will fail to achieve the desired results.[ii] Fortunately, we know why. Here are seven of the most common misguided efforts. Most communities will:

1. **Focus on external change, rather than the inner work.** Communities will focus on changing what's on the surface of their lives (e.g., buildings, finances, land, and ministries), and ignore what's underneath, the inner work of personal and interpersonal transformation.

2. **Make new improved versions of the past.** Just like the new improved versions of Tide or Crest, communities will make new improved version of themselves. They will attempt to do what they have always done, only better.

3. **Try harder, not differently.** Communities will try harder to tighten their belts, reduce expenses, postpone retirement, downsize, rightsize, and repurpose buildings, hoping for a different outcome (Einstein's definition of insanity).

4. **Play it safe, rather than innovate.** They will play it safe, rather than innovate, out of fear of making bad investments, losing their

reputations, or experimenting and failing. As it turns out, playing it safe is the riskiest choice of all.

5. **Engage in incremental, rather than deep change.** Communities favor small changes in which the outcomes are predictable, conversations are manageable, and things are more controllable, rather than choose to engage in deep change.

6. **Avoid something bad, rather than create something good.** Fear drives communities to worry more about making mistakes, rather than focusing their attention and resources on innovating new possibilities.

7. **Download the same information, rather than create a new operating system.** When communities get stuck in their same old mindsets and worldview, they end up downloading the same information using the same filters, rather than creating a new operating system. Without a transformation of consciousness (new operating system), no truly novel possibilities will emerge.

You may have noticed that *fear* is the common denominator among all of these misguided efforts. Leaders and members are afraid of genuine transformation because it is downright messy and painful. Transformation is inherently complex, conflictual, intimate, ambiguous, and risky and the results are always unpredictable. Most groups lack the courage, creativity and tenacity needed to engage in this kind of work. Most will focus on surface changes, the bricks and mortar of organizational change. They will eschew the pain and messiness of inner personal and interpersonal work. Instead, driven by fear, they will take the well-worn path of least resistance, a path that inevitably leads to slow decay and death.

A way forward

The path less taken, the path that transforms and brings forth new life for communities, necessitates not only organizational transformation, but also the inner work of personal and communal transformation. All three dimensions, organizational, personal, and interpersonal, must be addressed in order to transform a community. Without the soulwork of its members, efforts aimed at communal transformation will fail to achieve their desired results.

While most communities are well versed in methods for addressing the organizational dimension of change, most do not have the tools to aid them in addressing the personal and communal dimensions. This book addresses that gap. It provides a comprehensive set of reflections, and a recommended process for using them, designed for communities to address the personal and interpersonal dimensions of communal transformation.

FOR WHOM THIS GUIDE IS WRITTEN

As I said, I use the term "community" rather broadly for the purposes of this book. What I mean by community is any group, formal or informal, that has a common mission or purpose. This might be a religious community, like the Sisters of Mercy or the Society of Jesus (Jesuits). Or it might be a smaller community of faith or church. Leadership teams, boards and nonprofit organizations for whom mission (not money) is the bottom line would find this material beneficial. Basically, any intact group that is facing a crossroads and searching for ways to transform their lives and bring forth new life will find this material a valuable resource for their own transformative efforts.

For whom is this book not suited? If and when this is used by a community, like any communal endeavor, not everyone will be drawn to this type of work. Some might not resonate with my language for God, spirituality or the soul. Some will be afraid of the kind of depth and integration I am encouraging with regard to the spiritual and emotional dimensions of our lives. Some might see this inner work as unnecessary "navel gazing" that diverts their attention away from mission. And still others might think that you can plan for the future, as you have in the past, by writing a vision statement, creating a strategic plan, and carrying out its goals and objectives on a fixed timeline. For those who hold these perspectives, this book will be a stumbling block.

However, I believe that this guide will strike a chord among those who have come to realize that they are in an unsustainable and unacceptable situation and, therefore, must radically change their future. I believe it will resonate with those who have come to realize that they cannot do this work unilaterally or alone, but only through collaboration and partnership. It is written for those who are looking for a way through the inherent ambiguity and complexity of transforming their lives and shaping a future together. I hope it will speak to those who, rather than adapting to our world as it is, wish to transform themselves and the world in which we live.

Admittedly, a journey of communal transformation is inherently ambiguous, and progress is hard to measure. It is akin to a pilgrimage in that way, but with the added complication of its link to organizational change. Who can prescribe what is God's work in our life and by what yardstick can you measure such progress? How can you prove that the concrete organizational plans you implement actually spring from authentic communal discernment? This is a journey with few landmarks or worldly measures of success. It has more to do with the landscape of the soul. Only *you* can attest to the authenticity of God's presence in your inner journey, how this informs the paths you are choosing, the decisions you are making, and whether or not you are making any progress.

I cannot tell you exactly how to give renewed expressions to the soul of your community or its mission. I cannot offer you a prescription for guaranteed success. And I cannot put God into this journey for you. What I can do is provide you with a means to deeply reflect upon your life and engage in the inner work of transformation. What I can offer is a way for you to ponder who you are called to become, experiment with how to facilitate that new birth and begin to write a new narrative for your life. What I can give you is a way to go about this soulwork that has its foundation in the wisdom gathered from contemporary science and humanities, life experiences and numerous faith traditions.

Individuals without a community engaged in transformation

This guide would also benefit individuals who may not be in a community that is currently engaged in transformative efforts but nonetheless wish to do their own personal work of transformation. Ideally, you might create a peer group of likeminded individuals to join in this endeavor. This could be just one other person who is a significant other, a trusted confidant, a spiritual director or counselor. Or you might want to form a peer support group with others who share the same desire for personal transformation.

Having companions on the journey bolsters the transformative potential of this soulwork. The intimacy of what you share together intensifies its emotional impact. Having others who can "witness" your journey helps to affirm your work, solidify your gains and sanctify your growth. Your thoughts and feelings when spoken aloud will become more real, more internalized and owned by you. The contemplative nature of this material and the compassionate presence of others can offer much needed support, challenge and insight to aid in your work.

BENEFITS OF THIS GUIDE

This reflective guide offers two very specific benefits to those who work with it. When used with the suggested process that incorporates personal reflection and communal sharing this material will help you and your community engage in both the personal and communal work of transformation. In addition, it will help you build a "container" to manage the intrinsic chaos of transformation.

Inner personal and interpersonal work of transformation

Discernment is personal, but never private.
James Martin

This guide is intended to help you do the inner work of transformation, which is both personal (i.e., spiritual and emotional) as well as interpersonal (i.e., relational and communal). If you are to succeed in the work of communal transformation, each person in the community will need to engage in this kind of inner work, even though not everyone will do this work in-depth. However, the odds of communal transformation taking place will be increased to the degree that more of your members are engaged in this kind of in-depth work.

Let me be clear, the personal inner work of transformation must not remain private and siloed. Your efforts need to extend beyond the individual and into your relationships. You will need to engage in the interpersonal work of transforming normative patterns of relating that have previously led to silencing the inner voice of the community (e.g., judgmental ways of talking, wounds left unattended, conflicts avoided, leadership triangulated, blaming and shaming of those with whom we disagree, etc.). You will need to grow in your capacity for having honest, direct and meaningful conversations, reconciling wounds, restoring trust, and creating new norms that enable you to thrive.

If everyone did this work on their own or went to spiritual direction or counseling to do the work, it would not result in communal transformation. Unless and until this personal work is shared with the community, and worked through as a community, there will be no communal transformation. The community as a whole is a lifeform, a system with its own norms, culture and soul. It will not be transformed unless there are processes specifically aimed to address the system as a whole. Thus, the processes and reflections I am offering here for sharing among members is where the personal and interpersonal work come together, each complementing and aiding the other.

Build the container

Your sacred space is where you can find yourself over and over again.
Joseph Campbell

Using this guide will strengthen the "container" needed for your collective work of transformation. The container is a space wherein people experience:

1. a green space where they feel safe enough to risk, learn and grow together in community,

2. a sacred space wherein they can listen to and cooperate with the Spirit moving within and among them, and

3. a common understanding and framework for what they are doing.

A container is a type of holding environment. In order for you to engage in deep change, you must create a safe environment, a green space, in which to be vulnerable, to risk, and to experiment without fear of judgment or reprisal when you fail (and you will fail many times). You need a welcoming space, one hospitable to the soul, wherein you can be honest, intimate and real. Such a container becomes "sacred space" when your souls are attuned to the Spirit moving through your hearts, personally and collectively. You need the kind of milieu wherein you can grow in collective clarity about what you are doing and where you hope to go in the future.

Typically, any passion and clarity that might have come from a community's gathering begin to wane when the gathering ends. The collective memory fades and so too does the collective spirit of enthusiasm and hope. Gatherings then become isolated, one-and-done events that are disconnected from one another without a sense of integrating and building something whole. While a given gathering may be worthwhile, in and of itself the experience can remain siloed. This limits your ability to sustain momentum, build upon the steps taken, and integrate your ongoing efforts.

This guide provides a means for building and sustaining a common framework, a common understanding for what the community is doing and why. It is a way of strengthening the container and integrating the work in-between gatherings. It is a means to provide a continual rhythm of prayer and reflection so that everyone is involved, doing this work together, and moving in a common direction. It provides a shared sense of meaning and purpose to their transformative journey.

CONTENTS OF THIS GUIDE

Until we all reach unity in the faith and in the knowledge of the Son of God and become mature, attaining to the whole measure of the fullness of Christ.
Ephesians 4:13

This guide offers a series of 20 reflections and related meditative passages, prayers, journal exercises and rituals. Each reflection begins with an introduction to an element of the Journey of Transformation. I have also drawn upon scripture, prayers, poems and other inspirational sources to further enhance your engagement in the reflections. I will describe an approach you might use for working with these reflections individually, in small groups and as an entire community.

Part I, *Journey of Transformation*, provides the context and origins for the inner work of transformation. It describes the larger framework, the Journey of Transformation. It is a brief overview of some of the foundational learnings unearthed in the companion book, *Graced Crossroads: Pathways to Deep Change and Transformation*. It also describes the difference between change and transformation.

Part II, *Connecting Change with the Inner Work of Transformation*, explains the important connection between the outer work of change and the inner work of transformation. It explains the keys to unraveling the mystery of transformation, how we can do our part to participate in this Divine Mystery. It describes, also, the role of grace and how we can learn to cooperate with grace. The 20 reflections are then divided across the next four Parts.

Part III, *Graced Crossroads*, introduces the first set of reflections. These will invite you to reflect upon experiences of your own graced crossroads wherein you chose life in a profound way. You will be asked to recall those times in your life wherein you experienced an in-depth, life-changing and grace-filled transformation. You will be asked to explore questions, such as: What circumstances brought you to these graced crossroads? What was the deeper invitation and hidden wholeness? What did grace have to do with it, and what helped you to choose life through a path of transformation instead of taking a path of least resistance? You will then be invited to gather the learnings from your past experiences and apply these to the present. You may choose to explore a current crossroads in your own life and/or the current crossroads in your community.

Part IV, *Dynamic Elements of Transformation*, invites you to pray and reflect upon how you journeyed through transformation toward new life. These reflections are based on what I have identified as the five dynamic elements of transformation. They take you beyond the theory of transformation into your personal experience. For example, you will be asked: How were each of the five dynamic elements a part of your personal journey of transformation? How did you work with the ambiguity and confusion during that time? Who walked with you? How was your faith life a part of your journey?

Part V, *Life Review*, provides a way of clearing out the clutter that otherwise diminishes the radiant light of your soul: healing wounds, forgiving and being forgiven, grieving your losses in life, handling disappointments and regrets, and so on. You will be invited to reframe scarcity into abundance and live more in the fullness of gratitude. The road to a mature spiritual life and a healthy emotional life involves more than working in these few areas, but these are among the most common issues that will help you plumb the depths of your soul.

Part VI, *Writing a New Narrative*, involves shedding "old skins" representing identities that have outlived their usefulness and are no longer authentic. You will be invited to explore new beginnings, discover ways in which you might flourish, and write a new narrative for your future.

How to Use this Guide

One of the best gifts of a journal is that it gives you a place to show up.
Helen Cepero

Does it sound like a lot of work? It is. However, it is not a race nor is it constrained by a specified time period other than the time you allot for it. This is the kind of work that can take a lifetime. While the sequence of these reflections is intended to build upon and foster integration from one to the next, you might choose to work with them differently. It's up to you how much time you give to this and how you approach the work.

There are any number of processes that could be developed in order to use this material. However, as a departure point, let me recommend one approach that I have used successfully with a number of communities. You can then adapt these suggestions to fit your own circumstances. I want to share this process with you at the start so that you have it in mind as you are working with the material.

FOR LARGE COMMUNITIES

Organizing small groups

If you are working with this guide as a larger community, it is best to divide up the community into small groups. Given the complex mixture of your members' schedules, capacity to do this work, motivations and resistance, baggage with other members, and varying living circumstances, it might be best for leadership to arrange these small groups. Leadership can discuss all these matters in confidence and arrange the groups in ways that optimize their potential viability. Here are a few things to consider:

1. Groups of six or seven are usually best. Smaller groups, if one or two people are absent or particularly shy about sharing, can diminish the richness of conversation. With larger groups (eight or more) it becomes cumbersome to get everyone's voice into the conversation. Larger groups require more time for everyone to share and they make spontaneous, free-flowing conversations a bit too cumbersome.

2. Using existing intact groups may or may not be wise. An existing group, especially one whose norms of sharing might work against this kind of intimate sharing, may become highly problematic. It usually works best to shake things up and arrange for new groups. This helps to ease the resistance that can sometimes become entrenched in some intact groups.

3. Using new groups offers the opportunity for people who do not know one another that well to become very bonded. Novel groups starting from scratch to build trust together can become profoundly cohesive. It also strengthens confidence that if they can build trust in this new group, they can do the same in other circles, rather than stay wedded to the safety and familiarity of an existing group.

4. If these new groups have individuals with "baggage," who have avoided one another for years because of past wounds, this can be a great opportunity for healing. Now, having to sit face-to-face,

they may come to a newfound appreciation of one another, even reconciling old wounds. The only caveat might be to not place people together who have strong disdain or rifts that are "too hot to handle." This is a judgment call for those who arrange the groups.

5. Each group ought to have at least one person who is capable of convening and facilitating the group. Be sure to place some members who may have more difficult styles of interacting with the stronger conveners/facilitators.

6. It is important that those who take on the roles of convener or facilitator are also participants; one as equals among the others. Meaning, they share just as equally and vulnerably as anyone else. They are not set apart as the helpers or experts.

Convening the small groups

It is best to have leadership provide the guidance and instructions for the processes used by the small groups. They can convene the groups on a regular basis and organize the approach for using the reflective exercises.

The rhythm for each reflection works best for most groups when it is done every couple of months. Leadership can let the groups know when to begin a particular reflection. This way all of the groups stay somewhat in sync.

Leadership can also let you know what kinds of feedback, if any, they might like to receive from the small groups. This feedback can be integrated into the collective work of the community. In other words, leadership can reflect back to the community how the small group feedback influenced their planning with regard to the overall Journey of Transformation. They might share with the community how the feedback was instrumental in shaping the content and processes they use at assemblies, or how they see the transformation of the community evolving over time.

For smaller groups and teams

You might be using this material for leadership development, team building or among members of your church or peer group. Adjust these guidelines to fit your circumstances. You might want to establish a convener who would organize the group, as well as determine how and when the material would be shared. You may want to assign a facilitator for the group, who may or may not be the convener. You might want to rotate these roles within the group. The caution here is that not everyone has the skills needed for these roles. Discuss these options before you get started.

Steps in the process

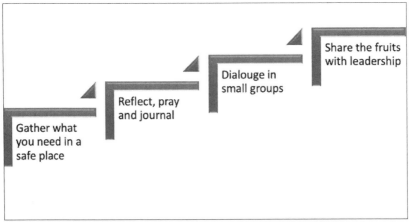

Figure 1: Steps in the process

Step one: Gather what you need and find a safe place

When instructed by leadership (or convener), gather your materials and find a sacred space of your own. You will need this guide and other spiritual readings of your choice.

Locate a safe, quiet, comfortable space that will help you introspect, pray, journal, and be with your God. You may already have such a space. You might wish to meet with a spiritual director or guide. You may wish to be among the healing spaces of nature or bring your work to retreats. It might help to begin each session with a blessing of that space in order to invoke the Sacred. Begin by getting centered. Breathe in the breath of God, the gift of life, and be still for a few minutes. Once you are ready, begin with the reflection and stay with it as long as it is useful.

Moses heard God's voice from a burning bush, saying, "Take off your shoes, for the earth on which you walk is holy ground" (Exodus 3:5). The ground on which your feet will be walking, the path of your life and your own journey of transformation, is also sacred. Honor it as sacred by the quality of presence you bring to this inner work of transformation. Begin and end your sessions with prayer.

Step two: Reflect upon, pray, journal and walk with your God

Read the assigned reflections and meditative materials. Spend time dwelling in deep prayer and introspection. Let your thoughts, feelings, and images emerge. Give it time. Let the reflections, quotes and questions sink into your soul. This is a process that unfolds over time, not in one sitting, so return to the same reflections on more than one occasion. Journal your responses by letting your words flow without regard for literary style, spelling or grammar. If the journaling takes you beyond the specific questions, then go there. Allow the questions to prompt, not limit, your writing. Above all, be honest and real.

Some of the exercises suggest the use of ritual. Some ideas are offered in this guide but, if you are not accustomed to creating your own rituals, you might ask for help from someone who is familiar with rituals. In addition, you may want to read some additional books and articles from the authors quoted in this guide if you find that they engage your soul and spark your imagination. You have the references and suggested readings in the back of this book. You may want to use some other medium to deepen your reflections (art, music, poetry, walking a labyrinth). Use whatever means you might like to help you reflect deeply upon the material.

Step three: Dialogue in small groups

Your spiritual journey is personal as well as relational. Bring your reflections to your small group and open up these intimate conversations as instructed

THE INNER WORK OF TRANSFORMATION

by leadership (or convener). The intimacy of this material is a powerful means for building community. Walk with one another as you share your insights. Listen deeply to one another as you walk this Emmaus journey together.

Leadership might invite you, at times, to share this material with your partners in mission or others small groups. Or you might be invited to share your work at assemblies. Don't let these invitations to share inhibit you from doing the personal work you need to do for yourself. You have a choice, in fact, the responsibility, in determining your own boundaries for what you share and with whom.

Step four: Offer your insights to the leadership

Leadership may find the responses to some of your reflections helpful in their ongoing planning with the community. They might wish to summarize responses to a particular reflection and share the summary with the community. Thus, you may be asked to share the fruits of your group's reflections with leadership. If this happens, and you wish to send them, be clear, concrete and descriptive in what you share, while honoring those who wish to keep their personal stories private. Determine as a small group what will (or will not) be shared with the leadership. Some of you might be willing to share your personal stories with leadership or at assemblies and others might find this to be too uncomfortable.

CREATING SACRED SPACE

Peeling the onion: How far to go?

Many people have tended to their internal life with the help of spiritual directors, counselors, or trusted confidants. Some have done this kind of work all of their lives, others sporadically, and still others may have shied away from this kind of work. This guide is intended to invite your spiritual and emotional growth in whatever way, at whatever starting point, and into whatever depth, you choose.

In asking you to reflect deeply upon your emotional and spiritual experiences of transformation, this will likely bring up some of the pain that was part of these experiences. Depending upon the depth and success of your prior work with these experiences, you might uncover some unhealed wounds or unanticipated and disturbing memories.

It will be important when you are doing these kinds of reflections that you respect your own limits and make personal choices about how much you want to explore. It may well be that such reflections provide a great opportunity for healing, but the choice needs to be yours as to just how far you go. You should not feel forced to face things you do not feel prepared to face. However, if you have a strong desire for in-depth explorations and deep healing, and your needed work seems beyond what the small group could provide by way of support or assistance, you might wish to do this work with a professional guide (e.g., counselor or spiritual director).

Sharing in community: How transparent should you be?

Given the intimate nature of these reflections, and the invitations to share these with others, you might feel unsafe. If so, talk about this with your small group before you begin. Talk about what you need from one another in order to feel safer in taking risks. Perhaps you've had a prior experience of a broken confidence, wherein what you thought was being shared privately was later shared with others. Perhaps you've had prior experiences of being harshly judged by others when you shared a deeply personal experience. Whatever your past experiences were, or your anticipated fears might be regarding the small group, discuss these and seek the assurances you need in order to feel safe.

Your dialogues with this material, while risky, are also intended to be the catalyst for transforming relationships that may have become unreconciled, stale, or superficial into ones that are more intimate and important. It may well be that such meaningful conversations release you from old wounds or painful reputations. Opportunities for reconciliation, understanding and healing can, and hopefully will, emerge. The intimate conversations that are invited through these processes can have a profound, transformative impact upon your individual and collective lives.

PRINCIPLES OF DIALOGUE AND COMMUNAL SHARING

Every community is different in their approach to how they dialogue and share on substantive topics. The practice of communal sharing must be tailored to a particular community and their specific goals. However, as an orientation to this kind of sharing, I usually offer these general guidelines.

1. *Embrace deeply your truest self* and unbind one another from the reputations that otherwise keep you hidden. Instead, seek to know one another as ever-awakening, yearning to be understood for who you are becoming.

2. *Tend to the garden* of your once treasured relationships by weeding out sources of mistrust or confusion and engage in skilled conversations that seek compassionate understanding.

3. *Listen, as if for the first time*, and not for what you expect to hear, are afraid to hear, wish to hear, or think you've already heard a hundred times before.

4. *Prepare your heart* to listen for the grain of truth among those hard-to-hear differences or pearls disguised as resistance or disagreement.

5. *Become captivated* by the heart of the matter and by the deeper story that is unfolding, rather than on superficial distractions and unrefined comments.

6. *Discover the themes* underneath the soundbites, as well as the universal struggles that all of us share by virtue of being human.

7. *Surrender* your need for quick fixes or pain-free answers and relish the gift of revelation in these soul-searching conversations.

8. *Savor the silence* and resist the urge to fill it with empty words and reactive comments.

9. *Listen to your inter-connectedness* with one another as companions on a shared journey.

10. ***Trust the wisdom of the community*** to call forth and glean the fruits of the Spirit moving within and among everyone gathered.

A no advice zone

These small groups are meant to be a "no advice zone." This is not group therapy. You are not there to tell each other what to do, problem solve, fix, advise or save one another. You are not there to pat one another on your backs for what we have done, or criticize, gripe or complain about what others have done. Nor are your reflections intended to be some kind of "faith sharing" wherein you might share, but others are not allowed to respond.

What's left if you can't advise, fix, problem solve or save? Your *presence*. You are being asked to listen, disclose and dialogue in a contemplative, yet interactive, manner. You are invited as mutual companions to be present to one another in your sharing. You are gathered as equals, no matter your title, position or expertise. You are there to deepen your personal and collective understanding of where the assigned material has taken you in your own reflections. Your undivided attention and genuine interest in one another, your deep listening and presence to one another, is what matters most.

You are asked to be active listeners, not passive listeners who occasionally might nod or utter, "Uh huh." Tell each other what you have heard each other say so that everyone knows what others have understood them to say. In other words, summarize or paraphrase, at times, what you've heard. Offer empathy by trying to capture the heart of the matter in what others are saying. Note especially the feeling words. Ask open ended questions to help the other person go deeper. Listen beyond the spoken word and offer hunches about what they have not yet said but what might be underneath. Most importantly, be *mutual* in response to what others share, challenging yourself to open up to others in a similar way to how they had opened up to you.

Do not let a personal disclosure go by without someone responding. It would be deadly to put out a personal reflection and hear nothing but crickets. Whatever safety the group may have developed up until then would surely evaporate. When we take a risk to share personally, and the response is silence, we can feel terribly unappreciated and exposed. Our fears of being judged or misunderstood begin to creep in and we project into the silent faces of others the worst of our fears. Don't let this happen. Respond to one another with what you understood each person to say and how you were affected. Then share in kind. Be mutual by offering your own vulnerability. No advice, experts or therapists allowed!

PART I:
JOURNEY
OF TRANSFORMATION

Unless a grain of wheat falls to the ground and dies, it remains but a single grain; but if it dies, it yields a rich harvest.
John 12:24

CONTEXT AND BEGINNINGS

So, what is this Journey of Transformation and what is the inner work that is so much a part of it? In order for you to better understand the context and origins for this inner work, let me first provide you with an overview of the Journey of Transformation and the difference between change and transformation. In Part II, I'll then discuss the importance of connecting the outer work of change with the inner work of transformation.

For over a half century all mainline religions, churches and affiliated communities in the northern hemisphere have been declining in numbers. Their members are fewer, older, and more frail. And, without an influx of new members, most will not survive. Because of demographic pressures alone, they can no longer continue doing what they have been doing in the past, at least not in the same way. Beyond a crisis of survival, they are experiencing a cascading set of other crises related to their identity, integrity and relevancy in the real world. There is no going back and the path they have been traveling has reached a crossroads.

This is the larger context and impetus that gave rise to the need for many communities to engage in efforts to either come to closure or create a new path to the future. Knowing they could not continue as they have in the past, many are searching for a new way forward. Sadly, most will go down the path of least resistance, hoping that their safe, small changes will make a difference, only to come to certain death. However, some, a smaller percentage, will muster the kind of courage, creativity and tenacity needed to make radical changes, transform their lives and give birth to a new way of being.

For decades I have accompanied communities at the crossroads, those who have sought to transform their lives and, in turn, the world. This ministry is not only profoundly meaningful and rewarding but is monumentally complex and challenging. One of the most challenging aspects is how to get an entire community onboard, with everyone pulling in the same direction and engaged collectively in the soulwork of transformation. The Journey of Transformation has been the approach I have developed and used to help communities understand the nature and purpose of communal transformation and how they can engage in this work.

A related challenge is how to help communities not only engage in the necessary planning for their land, buildings, leadership and finances, but how to connect the processes used to address these surface changes with processes aimed at deep change and transformation. The Journey of Transformation provides a way to do both. This approach connects and integrates the outer work of change with the inner work of transformation.

Over time, I began to craft materials and processes to help communities engage in shared reflections so that everyone is involved in the inner work, both the personal and interpersonal work of transformation. This inner work became a core component of the larger Journey of Transformation, the glue that held the members together. Many of these reflections are included in this book.

The wisdom unearthed from this inner work gave meaning and purpose to the outer work of planning and visioning. The surface changes were no longer changes made simply to rightsize buildings, improve their finances, or restructure their governance just to ease administrative burdens. These changes, with all of the letting go and sacrifice they required, became imbued with a sense of meaning and purpose that had sprung from deep inner work, the kinds of reflections and sharing you will be invited to do (i.e., grieving, shaping a legacy, healing wounds, claiming a new sense of home and belonging, thinking creatively and outside of the box, reframing scarcity into abundance, etc.).

The intimate nature of these processes connected members at a profound level, bolstering a sense of being-in-it-together. It strengthened community and prepared them emotionally to withstand the chaos of transformation. Because of what this inner work invited members to share, it helped them grow in understanding one another and heal from past wounds. Through the personal reflections and communal sharing, they were transformed both personally and as a community.

JOURNEY OF TRANSFORMATION: AN OVERVIEW

The Journey of Transformation is an approach to communal transformation that integrates the pragmatics of planning and visioning with processes aimed at deep change. The processes, taken as a whole, provide communities with a framework for collectively understanding their work of transformation and a container that holds communities together while encountering the necessary chaos. It is a multidimensional, multilayered and integrative approach. In essence, it is a communal faith journey with a two-fold aim: helping communities discern God's call to new life and transforming the meaning, purpose and lived expression of their community and its mission.

The Journey of Transformation provides a method and means for cooperating with grace through the Divine Mystery of transformation. While the inner workings of grace upon our soul will remain forever inscrutable, the human mystery of transformation is made more fathomable if we take into account: 1) the recent accumulation of knowledge through science and the humanities; 2) the insights gained from countless experiences of transformation that we have all had personally and witnessed in creation; and, 3) the kinds of pathways of transformation we know from ancient and contemporary faith traditions. It is on the basis of these three foundations that this Journey of Transformation has been predicated and developed.

Framework and container

The Journey of Transformation is, first of all, a framework for understanding communal transformation. Every member of your community likely has a different understanding of your current situation and different opinions about the needed approach for change or transformation. Without a common frame of reference, leaders and members will end up pulling in different directions. The Journey of Transformation provides a common framework for understanding what is at stake, the options before you, and how to engage in the work of communal transformation.

This framework for understanding also establishes a container, or holding environment, wherein members can journey together in their collective inner work of transformation. It provides a way for everyone to be on the same page as to what they are doing and why. This gives the community a way of orienting themselves and hanging together when the going gets tough and chaos ensues. They are more willing to stay in the struggle when the intimacy, ambiguity, conflict, and overall messiness of transformation evokes fear, anger, confusion and other uncomfortable, albeit necessary, emotions. The inner work and its messiness are made more manageable when everyone has a common understanding as to why it is so necessary to go through the chaos and how they can go through it together.

Multidimensional

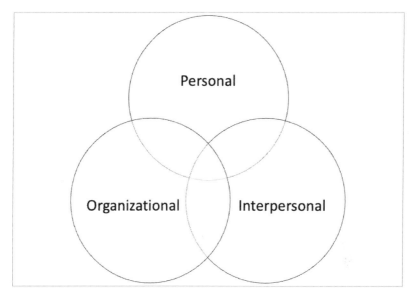

Figure 2: Multidimensional Transformation

The Journey of Transformation is multidimensional and holistic. It combines and integrates *personal* (i.e., emotional and spiritual), *interpersonal* (i.e., relational and communal), and *organizational* (i.e., structural and systemic) processes. For example, if any one of these three components is missing, then communal transformation will fail. If every member of your community sought spiritual direction or therapy, but collectively avoided the interpersonal or organizational dimensions, communal transformation would not occur. Similarly, if you sought to address the interpersonal dynamics in community, but avoided the personal or organizational dimensions, communal transformation would fail. And if you simply focused on organizational changes, but neglected the personal and interpersonal work, your efforts would fail. The vast majority of communities attend to the organizational changes but fail to address the personal and interpersonal dimensions.

Multilayered

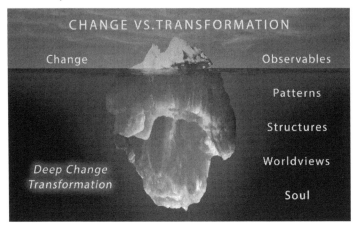

Figure 3: Change vs. Transformation

The Journey of Transformation is also multilayered. It addresses the visible realties and **observable** challenges facing communities that are evident on the surface of community life. These include, for example, land, buildings, finances, healthcare, ministries and demographics. These are the tangible dimensions of life that are typically addressed through conventional change processes. These external aspects of community must change in order to adapt to internal and external pressures. However, focusing only upon these external changes will not bring about transformation.

Communal transformation must also involve the less visible challenges related to patterns, structures, worldviews and the very soul of communities.

The **patterns** and practices within communities are less tangible and obvious than the observables, yet these shape how members understand who they are and what they are about. These are the normative ways in which a particular community orchestrates life (e.g., gathers, prays, makes decisions, forms members, builds trust, handles conflict, celebrates, grieves, shares information, manages boundaries, exerts power, uses authority, creates budgets, etc.). These practices include what is written in governing documents, as well as what is established by unwritten norms and traditions. Shifting patterns is much harder than making surface changes, yet this kind of deep change is key to transforming the culture of community.

Structures include those gatherings and groups that support a community's life as it is in the present or has been in the past. These are the forums for gathering (e.g., local communities, assemblies, clusters, etc.), governing structures (e.g., leadership, committees, boards, regions, provinces, etc.), and all of the offices in the organizational chart (e.g., finance, health care, formation, maintenance, development, communications, etc.). In order for a community to transform itself, it must *destructure* to make room for the spirit and, simultaneously, restructure to create new, more evolved and flexible structures aligned more fully with the future a community hopes to create.

Worldviews and mindsets include all of the prevailing ways of understanding life as it is in the present or has been in the past. It is expressed in the narratives of a community, in other words, how a community understands and tells its story. These stories are revealed through the myths, truths, untruths, assumptions and events that shape and explain life as it is today. These are filters that determine what is real, relevant or irrelevant in the lives of members. Worldviews and mindsets create the paradigm that shapes meaning and purpose for members, along with their core ideology and values that support the paradigm.

The **soul** of a community is analogous to the soul of an individual. The soul is the essence or inner voice of the community. The soul is the place where the Divine dwells deep within a community and it is the seat and source of life for a community. Transforming the soul of a community is a journey through the dark night where members confront the gap between who they say they are and how they live their lives.

If the external, pragmatic changes are made without integrating and addressing the internal, underlying elements in which these are embedded, there will be no transformation. For example, you can change where you live but, as they say in Alcoholics Anonymous, "you will take your patterns with you." In other words, you can change the size of your buildings, the lines and squares on your organizational chart, how you provide healthcare for your members, but you take your patterns, structures, and mindsets with you. Unless you do the inner work, your soul remains untouched and unchanged.

The Journey of Transformation to which I am referring not only seeks to change what is on the surface of your lives but to transform what lies beneath.

The deeper patterns, structures, worldviews and, indeed, the very culture and soul of a community must be transformed in order to bring forth greater wholeness and fullness of life. It is not the surface changes that will transform you but the deeper, inner work that ultimately transforms a community.

Integration and alignment

Figure 4: Realignment

The Journey of Transformation aims to realign life at all levels (see figure 4, *Realignment*). The goals here are: to better align the soul of community with its mission so that the two are more connected and integrated; to forge a vision that flows more directly from a community's mission; and establish directions that are more integrally linked to the vision. The overall purpose then is to align life at all levels so that a community becomes more relevant and responsive to the urgent and emergent needs of the world.

From a Christian perspective, the essence of this journey is the Paschal Mystery of life, death, resurrection and new life. It is a journey that builds upon the virtues of faith, hope and love. In this sense, it is more a pilgrimage than a plan, more about the sort of people you are becoming, than an effort to create some kind of grand vision. It is about coming home to God and one another. It is a journey in which Christ is formed in us and through our own lives so that we become agents of transformation for others and our world.

Thus, the Journey of Transformation is a multidimensional, multilayered and integrative approach. At a pragmatic level, it helps communities create a plan and vision for their future. At a deeper level, it helps communities listen and respond to the lure and love of God to make manifest their deepest longings. It is a journey that invites greater wholeness and authenticity among members while embracing such values as mutuality, shared power and collective wisdom. It demands great courage, creativity and forbearance, asking nothing less than a no-holds-barred, all-out effort of every member of community.

Difference between Change and Transformation

When we are no longer able to change a situation, we are challenged to change ourselves.
Victor Frankl

The journey I am describing is aimed at transformation, not simply change. These two terms, although often used synonymously, are qualitatively distinct phenomena. Among the most important distinctions are these:

1. Transformation is an internal process, while change is an external event;

2. Crisis inevitably leads to change but merely invites the possibility of transformation;

3. Transformation involves deep, not incremental, change; and,

4. Transformation is a life-long, spiraling, maturational movement.

Transformation is an internal process

Change is an *external event,* a new arrangement of things that we can see and touch on the surface of our lives. Transformation, on the other hand, is an *internal process* that brings about new patterns and perspectives in response to change. It is a process that takes place over time and not as a result of a one-and-done event. While transformation always involves change, the reverse is not necessarily true. Transformation is not a concept or idea out there; it is an inside-out, soul-to-surface, highly visceral experience.

You might change where you live, your ministry, your attire, your relationships, but you take your patterns and perspectives with you. Communities might change administrative structures or merge with another community, but they take their culture with them. Communities might downsize, sell property, hire lay management for their healthcare, but they take their existing language, assumptions and worldviews with them. Communities might change every conceivable aspect of their lives, but their soul remains untouched and unchanged *unless* they do the inner work of transformation.

Organizational change is not the same as organizational transformation. Changing the bricks and mortar of your lives is not enough to transform a community. Transformation involves inner work that engages members in deep change processes aimed at shifting the meaning and purpose of community and its mission, patterns, practices, structures, mind-sets, skill-sets and heart-sets, down to its very soul.

Crisis offers a deeper invitation

Crisis insists upon change and offers an opportunity to listen for a *deeper invitation*. A crisis by definition is an experience wherein our ability to cope is overwhelmed by challenging circumstances. The status quo no longer works. Our coping skills are maxed out and we are in such acute or chronic pain that we fall apart. We have what is euphemistically called a "breakdown." This breakdown is a necessary antecedent to transformation. We must break down before we can break though. However, transformation only occurs in the breakdown if we listen for a deeper invitation and make a conscious choice to pursue it.

When we break down we have an opportunity to break through, but it is not automatic and there are no guarantees. We have choices to make and work to do. We could simply change things by removing ourselves from the stressors, reducing the stressors, or learning new and more effective ways of coping with them. Alternatively, we might choose to listen to a deeper invitation. A crisis requires that we change and provides an invitation to transform, but the choice is always ours. Communities could choose simply to adapt or they might choose to discern what God is asking of them. The former leads inevitably to change, while the latter leads to the possibility of transformation.

Transformation involves deep change

Transformation is an experience of *deep* versus *incremental* change. Throughout most of our life we change gradually and incrementally, accumulating and honing our skills, gathering knowledge and understanding. However, these periods of relative stability and incremental change are periodically punctuated by deep change. Piaget called this episodic leap "accommodation." Gregory Bateson referred to it as "the difference that makes a difference." Communication theorists call it "second order change." When referring to organizations or cultures it is typically called systemic or paradigmatic change. In the language of faith, it is called conversion.

According to Robert Quinn, incremental change is rational, predictable and occurs in small linear steps. It is gradual, narrow in scope and reversible. It makes new and improved versions of the past, extending the past into the future. It is much more about holding on than letting go, and typically leads to entropy and slow death (unless countered in some way). Deep change, on the other hand, is intuitive. It occurs in sudden leaps and the results are unpredictable. It requires new thinking, is broad in scope and irreversible. It transcends and is discontinuous from the past. It is more about letting go and taking risks with a leap of faith.[iii]

Transformation is a life-long, spiraling, maturational movement

We grow in a spiraling motion with periodic leaps of maturation, self-transcendence and an expanding consciousness. We grow incrementally for extended periods of time and periodically go through a transformative process resulting in qualitative shifts in consciousness. These transformative leaps result in new levels of consciousness wherein we gain a wider, more inclusive perspective and see ourselves and our world in an entirely new way. These spiraling cycles of maturation and growth occur throughout our lifetime for as long as we choose to embrace their possibilities.

Systems theory and Spiral Dynamics show us how organizations and cultures change in a similar cyclical, spiraling fashion. The same transformative movements are observed in communities. David Nygren and Miriam Ukeritis, in their studies, said that communal transformation refers to "qualitative discontinuous shifts in the members' shared understandings of the organization, accompanied by changes in the organization's mission, strategy, and formal and informal structures."[iv] This spiraling cycle continues throughout a community's lifetime for as long as they choose to embrace these possibilities.

Thus, change and transformation are two very different and distinct phenomena. Most communities focus on change and give lip service to the deeper work. Both are necessary, though, and must be integrally connected in order for communal transformation to take place.

Let us turn now to explore the nature of transformation, its connection to change and how this soulwork provides a means for cooperating with grace.

PART II:
CONNECTING CHANGE WITH THE INNER WORK OF TRANSFORMATION

Groups made ornamental changes.... They changed their habits but not their hearts, their language but not their ideas.
Joan Chittister

INNER AND OUTER WORK

The Journey of Transformation *integrates* the outer work of organizational planning with the inner work of transformation. It integrates the strategic planning processes required of organizational change with the deep change processes required of transformation. These two distinctly different processes (strategic and aspirational) are woven together and combined to provide the method and means for communal transformation.

One of the most important lessons learned from studies related to psycho-therapy and personal healing is that symptom relief and surface changes are not the same as deep change and transformation. Even Weight Watchers has come to realize that weight loss by itself will not be sustained unless there is a change in lifestyle. Their new app no longer just counts calories for food intake. It teaches coping skills for stress reduction and even mindfulness. Personal transformation is an in-depth, soul-to-surface change process that promotes a new integration of our inner emotional and spiritual being, our values and beliefs, along with their outward behavioral expressions.

Lessons from studies on organizational change tell a similar story. Pragmatic surface changes, even structural changes, do not by themselves bring about transformation. Organizational change efforts fail to transform organizations if these neglect the inner work, which most do. Without addressing the deep culture in which these surface structures are embedded, namely, the norms, patterns, worldviews, and indeed the very soul of an organization, there will be no transformation.

For example, a community might merge with another community, reduce the number in leadership, rightsize buildings, or consolidate administra-tive offices, hoping to bring about some kind of transformation. Too often, leadership will initiate these efforts and attempt to frame them in a spiritual context, hoping their members will make a deeper connection and embrace it. But it doesn't work.

Simply overlaying spiritual language on top of what is essentially an organi-zational change process, without providing processes that explicitly integrate the two, has little substantive impact. Members aren't fooled. Rhetoric that is not backed up with processes that clearly link the concrete changes to the personal, interpersonal and organizational work of transformation has no lasting impact. Members have heard these speeches before and, having expe-rienced no lasting change, no real transformation or signs of new life, they become skeptical. They are no longer convinced or motivated by rhetoric to commit their time or energy to shallow, organizational changes.

Transformation does not take place as a result of a great speech, a great arti-cle or one-and-done assemblies. It does not fit neatly into artificial timelines, such as, leadership terms. It is an ongoing process of conversion that takes place over time as a result of a community's unwavering commitment, courage and creativity. *A key to communal transformation is to continually integrate the inner work of transformation that engages the hearts and souls of members with the outer work of change that addresses the community's concrete realities and plans for the future.*

KEYS TO THE MYSTERY

What the caterpillar calls the end, the rest of the world calls a butterfly.
Lao Tzu

If transformation is ultimately a Divine Mystery, how can we possibly understand it, let alone create processes to help it happen? What is our part to play, or are we left only to pray and hand things over to God?

In a 1939 radio broadcast, Winston Churchill said, "I cannot forecast to you the action of Russia. It is a riddle, wrapped in a mystery, inside an enigma; but perhaps there is a key." The same might be said of transformation. Its outcome cannot be forecasted. We never know ahead of time where it might lead. Transformation is a riddle wrapped in mystery. While the innermost workings of grace upon our soul will always remain mysterious, transformation itself is not completely obscured from our understanding. There are three keys to help us unravel this mystery:

- *empirical knowledge*, derived from recent advances in science and the humanities;

- *experiential knowledge*, gleaned from reflections on our own transformative experiences in life and witnessing those in creation; and,

- *soul knowledge*, cultivated through what we know from contemporary and ancient faith traditions and our own spiritual journeys.

We have partially unraveled this mystery through a vast accumulation of empirical knowledge. Modern studies in science and the humanities have shed light on the nature of transformation. There is more to it than alchemy and time. We also know of transformation through our own experiences of it. We witness and experience it throughout our lifetime. We can draw upon our experience to learn of its ways. We can draw upon our own spiritual journeys to add to this knowledge base. The rest, of course, is Mystery. It is left to faith, not a passive-dependent faith that hands everything over to God but a mature faith in which we do our part.

Let us unravel this human mystery of transformation as much as we can, because without some way of understanding it, we cannot intentionally plan for how to engage in the work of it. We cannot do our part if we do not know what is our part to play. Let us consolidate our three sets of knowledge-based learnings and reflect upon the role of grace in the mystery of transformation. This will help us know how we might proactively cooperate with grace.

A RIDDLE UNRAVELED BY CUMULATIVE EMPIRICAL KNOWLEDGE

We have developed as a species over our 250,000 years of existence. In the last century and a half, through advances in science and humanities, we have learned a great deal about human development. We have unearthed new understandings of deep change processes in humans and in organizations, as well as in communities and the cultures we create. Our knowledge of human development, understandings of systemic change, and what we now know of evolution and the story of the universe, has shed a great deal of light on this mystery of transformation.

TEN FOUNDATIONAL LEARNINGS

Taken together, what do these different disciplines of human, social, organizational, cultural and evolutionary development tell us about the nature of transformation? Let me offer a synthesis: ten essential lessons upon which the Journey of Transformation is predicated. Five lessons inform the *principles*, and five lessons inform the *dynamic elements*, which are concepts and processes incorporated into the Journey of Transformation.

Guiding principles

1.   Maturation is a lifelong opportunity

2.   Growth and transformation move in spirals

3.   We plateau for a time, then transform

4.   We breakdown to breakthrough

5.   Pain impels us, but love pulls us through

Dynamic elements

1.   Shifts in consciousness: creating a new narrative

2.   Reclaim our inner voice: the seat and source of everything that lives

3.   Reconciliation and conversion: the womb of our becoming

4.   Experimentation and learning: acting our way into a new way of being

5.   Transformative visioning: gather the wisdom, weave a dream

GUIDING PRINCIPLES OF TRANSFORMATION

Maturation is a lifelong journey

To exist is to change, to change is to mature, to mature is to go on creating oneself endlessly.
Henri Bergson

Maturation is a lifelong journey with endless opportunities to become more of who we are called to become. We are neither pre-formed at birth, nor do we stop growing at the end of puberty, at twenty-one, or ninety-one. Life is growth and growth is lifelong, *if* we choose it to be. Neither are we preprogrammed at birth, nor is our growth a given. Our maturation, our transformation and, ultimately, our destiny are the result of *choices* we make throughout our lifetime. The longer we live, the more opportunities we have to choose, but the choices are ours to make and there are no guarantees of success. At every crossroads there is an opportunity to grow, transform and become more of who God intends for us to be.

Carl Jung once said, "The privilege of a lifetime is to become who you truly are." In other words, aging is not the same as maturation. Your age only tells us how long you've lasted, but it says nothing about how much you've risked to grow, love, stumble, forgive, grieve, create or care for others. How many times you've failed in these efforts matters less than how many times you've gotten back up and what you've learned. In the end, it matters less how long you've lived than it does how fully you've lived, and how faithful you've been to who you were called to become.

Growth and transformation move in spirals

One of the chief beauties of the spiral as an imaginative concept is that it is always growing, yet never covering the same ground, so that it is not merely an explanation of the past, but it is also a prophecy of the future; and while it defines and illuminates what has already happened, it is also leading constantly to new discoveries.
Theodore Andrea Cook

We grow and transform in an inward, outward and *upward spiraling manner.* Scientists and seekers, alike, are discovering what ancient traditions have always known: life is an unending, spiraling journey toward the Divine. Each transformative turn of the spiral is a movement of growth that brings us to another developmental plateau and new possibilities. Life can be smooth sailing for a time, but it doesn't remain that way for long. The river of life is always changing and unfolding. It never stands still, repeats or goes backward. Our seasons in life may appear to repeat themselves, but only in general. No one season is a carbon copy of the last.

We have stages, phases and cycles, all moving along a spiral. We descend inwardly toward greater depth and wisdom. We grow outwardly, caring more about others and the world in which we live with greater capacity for empathy, love and appreciation of beauty. We ascend upwardly, subsuming and transcending prior developmental phases, thus enlarging our capacity for a more nuanced morality and fullness of life. Our spiraling growth is dynamic. It is an inside-out, soul-to-surface, future-oriented and open-ended movement, a teleological trajectory toward a greater union with the God ahead.

We must honor each stage, phase or movement throughout the journey. As we move up the spiral, with each new level of maturity, it is important to honor the prior levels. Each level is necessary and right for its time. We need to honor each level for what it is and not judge one as *better* or *worse* than another, any more than we would judge a 7-year-old as better than a 3-year-old, or one season of life as better than another. There are constraints, gifts, challenges and wisdom at every level and all are a part of the ongoing spiral of growth and transformation.

We plateau for a time, then transform

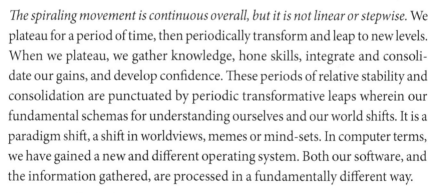

> *We must be willing to let go of the life we have planned, so as to have the life that is waiting for us.*
> E.M. Forster

The spiraling movement is continuous overall, but it is not linear or stepwise. We plateau for a period of time, then periodically transform and leap to new levels. When we plateau, we gather knowledge, hone skills, integrate and consolidate our gains, and develop confidence. These periods of relative stability and consolidation are punctuated by periodic transformative leaps wherein our fundamental schemas for understanding ourselves and our world shifts. It is a paradigm shift, a shift in worldviews, memes or mind-sets. In computer terms, we have gained a new and different operating system. Both our software, and the information gathered, are processed in a fundamentally different way.

We grow in fits and starts. Phases might awaken, surge, fade, merge, regress or transcend, but are never eliminated. Though we might be predominantly in one phase, we are never purely in one phase. Often, we exist in a blurred mixture of overlapping phases. We can regress a phase or two, but we can never skip a phase or two. Regression takes us back to old ways. Ideally, it would be a roundtrip, giving us a chance to loop back and reintegrate what was not integrated successfully before. For example, a current loss might trigger prior losses, ones which were not grieved successfully in the past. This gives us a chance to revisit our grief in a new way. With greater maturity, we can grieve our losses, old and new, with greater integration and resolution.

We breakdown to breakthrough

> *Whoever finds their life will lose it, and whoever loses their life*
> *for my sake will find it.*
> Matthew 10:39

It is nature's way, one of life's most agonizing paradoxes, that we breakdown to breakthrough. We have to fall down to grow up. We have to die in some way, let go of some treasured person, place, thing, belief, or way of life, in order to make the turn. Life and death, light and darkness, yin and yang, are artificial and illusory bifurcations of an unpartitionable whole. Death paves the way for resurrection, a transformation that is as messy and painful to personally experience as it is beautiful and exciting to witness in others and in creation. We fret and agonize through the dying on the front end of transformation, yet we find liberation and new life on the other side.

Life is not a game of perfect, but a game of recovery. We are all fragile. We all fall and fail and make mistakes. And all of these are necessary for us to grow. Crisis and breakdown precede and provoke transformation. There is no way around it: "No pain, no gain." It is nature's way. If there is no death, there will be no metamorphosis, no new life, and no future. We must lose our self in order to find our self once more (Matthew 10:39).

The degree of success to which an individual passes from one phase to the next influences how well he or she might move through subsequent phases. Successful breakthroughs to each new phase strengthen our capacity and bolster our confidence to make the passage through to the next developmental hurdle. However, phases and passages that are incomplete or unsuccessful carry the residual doubts and unfinished business into subsequent ones. Failures or fixations encumber us, but we are not doomed as damaged goods. Healing, repair work, recovery, and redemption can take place anytime throughout our entire lifetime. It's never too late!

Pain brings us to the crossroads, but Love pulls us through

Therefore, I am now going to allure her; I will lead her into the wilderness and speak tenderly to her.
Hosea 2:14

It is pain that brings us to the crossroads, but it is Love that pulls us through. Mounting internal and external pressures in life provoke and, eventually, force us to change. Pain and suffering bring us to the threshold of transformation, but it is Love that impels us through to the other side. God lures us into the wilderness. And it is both through our efforts and in our cooperation with grace, that we are truly transformed. Transformation requires both the stick (suffering) to push us to the crossroads, and the carrot (Love) to pull us through to the other side. Pain gnaws at us to relinquish our complacency and move, and Love points us to where we long to go. Suffering holds our feet to the fire until we finally let go, and let die what needs to die, in order to allow Love to awaken us, compassion to carry us, and grace to transform us.

At a graced crossroads, we are lured by God into the crucible of transformation. The pain that we want so badly to go away cracks open the shell of our psychological armor, hardened hearts and hubris. The shell that has protected us has also prevented us from experiencing God's grace. These painful come-to-Jesus moments are a necessary suffering because it breaks the shell open, allowing God's grace to break through. The pain that we so desperately want to escape, the pain that got us into this mess to begin with, and for which we want answers, is never answered in the way we expect. What we receive, instead, is grace and answers we could not have previously understood or conceived. It is, ultimately, through Love that we can withstand the pain of letting go, make meaning of the pain, and transform our suffering, so that new life can emerge.

DYNAMIC ELEMENTS OF TRANSFORMATION

Shifts in Consciousness: Creating a new narrative

> *With every move we make… we're dictating the next few lines of the text*
> *called our lives, composing it as we go.*
> Mary Catherine Bateson

Each developmental leap constitutes a shift or transformation of consciousness and opens the door for a new narrative in our lives. Each new turn creates in us a new consciousness and a new way of being. This transformation of consciousness vaults us higher into the spiral, and we grow into greater sophistication. Intellectually, we can grasp more complex ideas, nuance, irony and paradox. Relationally, we gain greater empathy and appreciation for more socially complex situations and moral nuances.

Gradually, we mature through an accumulation of knowledge and with each transformative leap we grow in wisdom. In each turn of the spiral we move beyond the confines of outdated paradigms. We move the boundaries of our own mental fences to encompass a wider landscape and a new worldview. The evolution of the brain gave us the cerebral cortex, capable of leaping us from prose to poetry, from basic math to quantum physics, from playing scales on the piano to playing Brahms. The evolution of human consciousness gave us the capability to leap from tribal instincts to altruism, and from egocentric to worldcentric perspectives and from either/or ways of thinking to awakening our hidden wholeness.

Include and *transcend* is the constant refrain in every turn of the spiral. Each new turn gathers up and carries with it all that preceded it, including, transforming and transcending all that was. The law of the universe assures us that nothing is lost. No prior memories and none of life's existence or energies are lost. They are subsumed and transcended, re-organized and re-integrated, transformed and made new, but never lost or left behind. All that ever was, still is. All that ever was, is now and not yet. We, and our universe, are works in progress, constantly transforming, transcending and including what was before into something even greater, the eternal story always unfolding.

Reclaim our Inner Voice: The seat and source of everything that lives

> *There is in all visible things … a hidden wholeness.*
> Thomas Merton

In every turn of the spiral, every maturational leap, we shed worn out vestiges of ourselves and claim anew our own inner voice, the seat and source of everything that lives. With every turn, layers of our false self are sloughed off. We turn inward again to the soul-truth of who we are, until our true self emerges anew. Every turn is our soul's homecoming, a return to our hidden wholeness. We return to the hidden source of life and become more fully who we are meant to be, more fully who God beckons us to be. We are drawn to *the more*, to that primordial ache to come home. And we can come home, more alive, more whole, more fully ourselves than before.

As we mature, we grow in our uniqueness and complexity. We individuate, differentiate, and distinguish ourselves from the herd. We grow in our truth and in our capacity to speak it. We grow more comfortable in our own skin, more secure and grounded in ourselves, helping us to better hear and be influenced by the truth of others. When we are younger, we want to try it all. We want the sampler plate. But, as my 101-year-old step-father likes to say, "At my age, I know what I like and don't like." We grow in knowing our likes, in claiming our wants and needs, and in discovering our gifts and talents. In so doing, the universe grows with us. The universe seeks diversity over sameness and creativity over conformity. It grows in and through the panoply of diversity brought forth by each lifeform claiming its uniqueness and maturing into fullness.

Reconciliation and Conversion: The womb of our becoming

Wholeness does not mean perfection – it means embracing brokenness as an integral part of life.
Parker Palmer

We spiral toward greater wholeness and connection through reconciliation and conversion, the womb of our becoming. The universe has an appetite for wholeness. Call it autopoiesis, if you like, but we have a built-in self-organizing drive and an innate capacity to move toward unity and wholeness. We don't like missing pieces in our jigsaw puzzles, things left hanging, or tensions unresolved. We want things whole, resolved, connected and completed. Hence, each turn of the spiral is a process of reconciling, reconnecting and reintegrating what has otherwise been broken or disconnected. The process of reconciliation and conversion is the very crucible of transformation where we are forged anew.

All forms of life, each in their uniqueness, are strands in the fragile web of life, parts of a whole, not siloed and separate but braided together. It is only in our illusion of separateness, and in the brokenness we create, that this gossamer web seems to fray. We are interdependent with all that exists. No life lives alone – not a cell, a person, a nation or a planet. When we are transformed into a new level on the spiral, we can see that more clearly. We move from self-centeredness to empathy, compassion, generativity and altruistic concern for others. We grow in concern for the web of life, our common home. We become more desirous and capable of intimacy, more aware that we are all in this together.

As we move up the spiral, we can see more clearly and poignantly that we are called to deeper conversion and healing. Each transformative leap is an exercise in reconciliation, restoring wholeness, and healing wounds that have kept us apart and damaged the web of life. The more we mature, the more we can embrace diversity and build bridges of understanding. We become more capable of mutually exchanging ideas, energies and talents with others, without losing our own identity. We are transformed in and through our reconciled relationships with others and, in so doing, we restore the fragile web of life.

Experimentation and Learning: Acting our way into a new way of being

First there is the fall, and then we recover from the fall. Both
are the mercy of God!
Lady Julian of Norwich

Each new turn of the spiral demands experimentation and learning, requiring us
to act our way into a new way of being. We have no clear picture, no clear path
and no guarantees of success as we grope and intuit our way forward. We live
our lives forward but understand them backward. Once we climb to a higher
vista, we can look back and see where we have been. When we go through a
new passage, it is always a leap of faith, and it always involves risk. If we try to
reduce the risk by insisting upon an ending of our own design, we only bring
more suffering. We cannot predict, engineer or control the outcome of transformative experiences. That is what makes it all so terribly unnerving. That is
why Joseph Campbell referred to it is an heroic journey.

When we are first growing into a new phase, groping and clamoring to reach
the other side, we stand on spindly legs. We do not yet fully understand nor
are we fully equipped for this new phase of development. We have to become
learners again by adopting a beginner's mind. We have to experiment with and
acquire new mind-sets, skill-sets and heart-sets. We have to fail and fumble.
Gradually, we accumulate knowledge, refine and master our skills, and gain
more solid footing in this new phase. It is, as Teilhard de Chardin taught us,
evolution in action.

Transformative Visioning: Gather the wisdom, weave a dream

I would love to live like a river flows, carried by the
surprise of its own unfolding.
John O'Donohue

Each new turn in the spiral is a process of transformative visioning where we gather the wisdom and weave a new dream. Each new turn in the spiral twists the kaleidoscope and brings into view an entirely new picture. The elements inside the kaleidoscope are the same – a mixture of our realities and our deepest longings – but when newly transformed and arranged, they create a new vision. When we reach a crossroads, we cannot see the vision of the future unfolding ahead of time. We can't know ahead of time what life will be like with all of its twists and turns. We are, instead, carried along by our hopes and dreams, carried by the surprise of its own unfolding.

The vision of the future is not one we can manufacture to our exact specifications. It is organic, emergent and iterative. It is *organic*, derived from life, not artificially engineered. It is *emergent*, showing only a glimpse of itself as we move along, each step taken revealing the *next best step* to take. We can't know ahead of time, what will be on the other side any more than a caterpillar knows that it will become a butterfly. It is *iterative*, in that we articulate one version, then another, each time adding clarity, texture, wholeness and depth. It is as if we begin a turn along the spiral, holding only a few small pieces of stained-glass window. Over time, we gather more pieces. More is revealed until an entire mosaic, like the rose glass of Notre Dame, comes into full view.

AN ENIGMA UNWRAPPED BY EXPERIENTIAL KNOWLEDGE

The most beautiful thing we can experience is the mysterious. It is the source of all true art and science. He to whom the emotion is a stranger, who can no longer pause to wonder and stand wrapped in awe, is as good as dead; his eyes are closed. The insight into the mystery of life, coupled though it be with fear, has also given rise to religion. To know what is impenetrable to us really exists, manifesting itself as the highest wisdom and the most radiant beauty, which our dull faculties can comprehend only in their most primitive forms-this knowledge, this feeling is at the center of true religiousness.
Albert Einstein

Adding to our empirical knowledge base, the ten foundational learnings, is our own experiential knowledge of transformation. Transformation of life, through death and the birthing of new life, is so common an experience that we can sometimes fail to notice, or know our part in, this astonishing mystery. It is a mystery hidden in plain sight. Death has never had the last word. It is *always* a new beginning. Every new beginning is always some other beginning's end. This mystery is so ubiquitous, though, we can lose sight of the miracle it truly is: the diurnal movement from dusk into darkness and from darkness into dawn; seeds that bud, bloom, die and return to life again next spring; the metamorphosis of the caterpillar into a butterfly or an embryo into an infant; the death of innocence and birthing of wisdom; the loss of someone or something we loved, opening a doorway to someone or something new.

We have lived through transformative experiences repeatedly over the course of our lives. We know of this mystery, and we know of the inner work of transformation, when we move through our own dark night experiences. We know of it when we suffered an emotional or spiritual crisis, lost someone or something we could never imagine losing, only to emerge again as new, more compassionate, wiser and more alive than before. We know of it when we have been called by a deep love that lures us out of our dull existence into one with meaning, purpose and passion. We know of it when we have transformed tragedy into triumph, conflict into creativity, and suffering into compassion. Throughout our lifetime we have countless experiences of endings (large and small) leading to new life.

Although we will get to these kinds of reflections in an in-depth manner later in this book, reflect for just a moment upon your own experiences of transformation. The most obvious example of this for religious men and women might be your vocational call to Religious Life. Or for laypersons, reflect upon your call to a particular ministry, to marriage or to another vowed commitment.

When you made these kinds of commitments, these leaps of faith, you did not simply change your address or your title. You changed your rhythm and patterns in life, the ways in which you celebrated, grieved, prayed and made decisions. You changed your primary relationships in life. You changed your relationship with God and the very meaning and purpose of your life. Your identity shifted profoundly. You were completely, radically and forever transformed, your soul enlivened in an entirely new way.

If you reflect upon an experience of transformation you've had in your own life, you will recognize that you had a hand in it. It didn't just happen to you. You actively participated in transforming your life. You did your own inner work to get through it. You relied on others and on grace to help you.

If we reflect upon our own past experiences, we can see how we had to deliberately let go of the old to make room for the new. We can see how we grew and transformed in ways that were transcendent. We can see how we preserved the core of our identity, while shedding old mind-sets, heart-sets and skill-sets in favor of new ones. We can see with each developmental leap in our lives that we moved to a new level of consciousness that was wider in its acceptance of diversity, more capable of empathy and interdependence, more nuanced in its morality. The mystery of transformation is made more understandable in the light of our own lived experiences and the insights these provide.

SOUL-KNOWLEDGE: A DIVINE MYSTERY KNOWN BY FAITH

The great heresy has been to turn faith's darkness into certitude. There is no wonder, no astonishment, no awe, no humility. There is no Mystery.
Richard Rohr

Transformation is a mystery understood partially from experiential and empirical knowledge. But at the end of all our experiential and empirical knowledge, at the end of all reason, transformation is a mystery we know by faith. Where knowledge and experience leave off, faith helps us walk the pilgrimage of transformation. Just when we thought we had all the answers; somebody changes the questions. When we are brought to a crossroads, the life we have known begins to break down. The breakdown serves a purpose. We are stripped of all pretense, emptied of all hubris and hollowed out for a reason. This hollowing out (*kenosis*) makes us more amenable to the workings of grace and the inbreaking of God's covenant love.

Think back to a crisis you experienced in life, the kind of crisis that brought you to your knees. These kinds of come-to-Jesus moments bring us to a crossroads in which going back to where we were is no longer an option, and the way forward seems impossible to fathom. This is where we step out in faith. Edward Teller describes it well: "When you come to the end of all the light you know, and it's time to step into the darkness of the unknown, faith is knowing that one of two things shall happen: Either you will be given something solid to stand on or you will be taught to fly."[v]

Reflect for a moment on the role your faith has played throughout these transformative experiences. Recall the ways your faith carried you through when reason no longer could. Reflect upon what your faith taught you about the nature of transformation, about your role and the role of grace. This is the knowledge, the wisdom, we know in our soul.

Stepping out in faith does not occur without our own volition and we are not transformed without our own arduous inner work. These experiences do not just happen to us. We do not move through these crossroads as passive bystanders being carried along by grace or as marionettes whose strings are pulled by some puppeteer god. Good intentions are not enough to transform us. Prayers alone will not transform us. We have to act. We have our part to do, our inner work, and pray that our actions are in accord with grace. We pray that God is companioning us along the way. We have to learn how to act in cooperation with grace, the very praxis of faith – the inner work of transformation.

COOPERATING WITH GRACE THROUGH THE INNER WORK OF TRANSFORMATION

And I said to the man who stood at the gate of the year: "Give me a light that I may tread safely into the unknown." And he replied: "Go out into the darkness and put your hand into the Hand of God. That shall be to you better than light and safer than a known way."
Minnie Haskins

Thus, transformation is partly a Divine Mystery, forever inscrutable and dependent upon grace. And it is partly a human mystery that we increasingly understand through an accumulation of empirical knowledge, insights from our own transformative experiences and our own soul's knowledge we come to by faith. It is this human part that depends upon our active participation, our own hard work, our willingness and ability to cooperate with grace. But how do we cooperate with grace? How do we dispose ourselves to the workings of grace?

The five dynamic elements described earlier are the primary ways for us to engage in the inner work of transformation. These key processes, when combined and woven together, provide the method and the means for cooperating with grace. These are the dynamic elements, or key processes, that inform the Journey of Transformation:

1. Shifts in Consciousness: creating a new narrative

2. Reclaim our inner voice: the seat and source of everything that lives

3. Reconciliation and conversion: the womb of our becoming

4. Experimentation and learning: acting our way into a new way of being

5. Transformative visioning: gather the wisdom, weave a dream

Your community can shift its resources, but it will not be transformed without a *shift in consciousness.* You can write your mission and visions statements, but without *reclaiming your inner voice*, these words will not hold the authenticity, passion and ownership needed among your members to make them real. Your community can try to avoid the tensions and conflicts that are a part of any human organization, but it will not become whole without doing the heart-work of *reconciliation and conversion.* You will not give birth to new life unless you become a learning community willing to risk, *experiment and learn* new mind-sets, heart-sets and skill-sets to support it. You will not *transform your vision* for the future unless you listen to the lure and love of God and give voice to your deepest longings.

These dynamic elements represent the core of the inner work of transformation, the type of work individuals and communities must do in order to cooperate with grace and participate in the Divine Mystery of life, death and resurrection to new life. None of these elements stand alone. They need to be translated into processes that interweave and connect each of these elements. The combined, dynamic movement of all five of these processes is what gives rise to a new life and a new way of being in the world. Your success will depend heavily upon the courage, commitment and creativity you bring to these processes. The rest is grace.

DISPOSED TO GRACE THROUGH THE VIRTUES OF FAITH, HOPE AND LOVE

Love is the true goal, but faith is the process of getting there, and hope is the willingness to live without resolution or closure.
Richard Rohr

We can do our part to cooperate with grace but how do we dispose ourselves to the workings of grace? How can we carry ourselves throughout the Journey of Transformation in a manner that we become more amenable to grace, so that grace can enter in? According to John of the Cross, the best way to carry ourselves through the dark night is in a manner that deepens the virtues of faith, hope and love. In other words, we dispose ourselves to grace by nourishing the virtues of faith, hope and love, the greatest of which is love (1 Corinthians 13:13).

Disposed to grace through faith

Reason is in fact the path to faith, and faith takes over when reason can say no more.
Thomas Merton

We make ourselves more amenable to grace when we walk in faith. We dispose ourselves to grace by listening to God, counting on God's covenant to be with

59

us and by doing what makes sense. "Faith is the assurance of things hoped for, the conviction of things not seen" (Hebrews 11.1.) With the eyesight of faith, what might God be saying to you? What do your current demands for change say to you about a deeper invitation? Are you listening, discerning and doing what makes sense, doing what might bring a smile to God's face?

Thomas Merton asked the same kinds of questions you are asking, and they brought him to this now familiar and fitting prayer:

"My Lord God, I have no idea where I am going. I do not see the road ahead of me. I cannot know for certain where it will end. Nor do I really know myself, and the fact that I think that I am following your will does not mean that I am actually doing so. But I believe that the desire to please you does in fact please you. And I hope I have that desire in all that I am doing. I hope that I will never do anything apart from that desire. And I know that if I do this you will lead me by the right road, though I may know nothing about it. Therefore will I trust you always, though I may seem to be lost and in the shadow of death. I will not fear, for you are ever with me, and you will never leave me to face my perils alone."[vi]

You might not ever see the results of your labor, but I know, as people of faith, you have the desire to please God. This journey is led more by faith and a desire to please God, than by strategic plans and reasoned agendas. There is no off-the-shelf plan, seven-point program or sure path to success. The path you'll need to take is the one you make as you go. It is made by taking one step at a time, pausing, discerning and choosing the next best step. We cooperate with grace through our faith, through our listening and discerning: "By day the LORD went ahead of them in a pillar of cloud to guide them on their way and by night in a pillar of fire to give them light, so that they could travel by day or night" (Exodus 13:21).

We have heard it time and again that the journey itself is the destination or, as some people say, how you get there is where you arrive. It is about how we journey together and who we are becoming along the way. It is about becoming more authentic, reconciled, grace-filled and passionately engaged in the fullness and joy of life. It is about becoming more of who we are meant to become, images of God, Love incarnate. That's the end game!

Moses never made it to the promised land, although, while sitting beside God, from across the way, he had a glimpse of it. We may never make it to the promised land in our lifetime either; although we too have had glimpses. And it is these glimpses, though fleeting, that renew our faith. It is in these fleeting moments, when we are sitting with God sharing our deepest longings that we are comforted by God's love, assured of the path we are on, and strengthened in our faith to keep going.

When we dispose ourselves to grace in this way, we are assured of God's covenant and promise of new life. *God's covenant is unwavering*: "When you pass through the waters, I will be with you; and when you pass through the rivers, they will not sweep over you. When you walk through the fire, you will not be burned; the flames will not set you ablaze." (Isaiah 43:2). *God's promise is unequivocal.* God's promise to Moses, the Israelites and their descendants, and to those of us who follow God in faith, is that we will be saved (Exodus 19-34). Persons and communities who cooperate with grace by being resolute in their faith will be accompanied by God and assured of new life, perhaps not within our preferred timetable, perhaps not in the ways we imagined, but surely within God's.

Disposed to grace through hope

Hope begins where optimism ends.
Sandra Schneiders

We open ourselves to the ways of grace through a *hope that knows of a future just beyond our grasp, but well within our reach*. While you will have your goals and desired outcomes, the Journey of Transformation does not rest on these alone. It rests also and especially in a hope that relies upon God's promise of new life.

This type of hope is not an over-spiritualized wishful thinking or an attempt to look at life through rose-colored glasses. It is about taking a long, loving look at the real, seeing its challenges and opportunities, and knowing that in the hardship we are not alone. It is experiencing, even in the seeming impossibility of it all, a complete trust in God's providence. This is not a passive-dependent reliance upon God, or a release from personal responsibility. It is an active hope that requires our responsible participation and partnership with God and one another to make it real.

Marcia Allen's outgoing presidential address at the Leadership Conference for Women Religious (LCWR) was entitled *Transformation – An Experiment in Hope*. She said, "We are wrapped in a sense of futility, doing more of the same in a most tiresome and enervating way…the status quo prevails…. After all the rational has been tried; after the solutions have been articulated and failed; when old language turns to ashes in our mouths, then we are reduced to silence. That is when hope is activated."[vii] That is when we are most amenable to God's grace and responsive to the alluring love of God.

This work of transformation and your fidelity to your life's commitments cannot be tied to the hope for results. Thomas Merton knew that when he prayed only to please God. In the now famous prayer written to commemorate Oscar Romero, *A Future Not our Own*, we are encouraged to take the long view: "We may never see the end results, but that is the difference between the master builder and the worker."[viii] Václav Havel grasped its essence when he said that hope "is not the conviction that something will turn out well but the certainty that something makes sense, regardless of how it turns out."[ix]

Joan Chittister, in her book *Scarred by Struggle, Transformed by Hope*, tells us, "There is no one who does not go down into the darkness where the waters do not flow and we starve for want of hope."[x] Yet in the starvation, in the struggle itself, lies the seedbed for hope. Hope emerges through the process of conversion. We are transformed and our transformation, she says, "brings total metamorphosis of soul."[xi] We all know this place, the place where we are forged in this darkness and transformed by hope emerging through the struggle. Hope enables us to endure the darkness, prevail in the struggle and transform our soul.

Is there hope for your community? There is hope for the future as long as your hope is an active hope, not just a passive hope made of prayers alone. In their book, *Active Hope*,[xii] Joanna Macy and Chris Johnstone highlight the difference between hope as something we *have* as distinct from hope as something we *do*. They stress the need to not only have hope but to do our part to bring it to fruition. Acting in hope on behalf of your community will dispose you to the workings of grace.

Disposed to grace through love

No eye has seen, no ear has heard, and no mind has imagined what God has prepared for those who love him.
1 Corinthians 2:9

Tina Turner asks, "What's love got to do with it?" After all, it's a "second-hand emotion," a "sweet old fashioned notion." "Who needs a heart when a heart can be broken?"[xiii] Love and heartbreak have a great deal to do with transformation. Love and heartbreak both make us amenable to the workings of grace.

Richard Rohr believes there are two great forces that aid in our transformation: "great love and great suffering."[xiv] I couldn't agree more. It is great suffering that compels, pushes and forces us to change and transform our lives. Great suffering breaks us down and hollows us out. It brings us to our knees and eventually to a crossroads, the threshold of transformation. But it is love that pulls us through. It is love that impels, lures, entices us to transform our lives. It sustains us in the struggle and obliges us to reach beyond. It is the combined effect of this push-me, pull-me dynamic of heartbreak and love that transforms us.

It is not love that brings people to therapy. It is pain. It is pain that gets us in the door, but it is love that heals and pulls us through. The studies on the effectiveness of psychotherapy, comparing one approach to another, all end up with the same conclusion. While certain techniques are more or less effective for specific disorders, the fundamental healing agent for all approaches is *compassion*. In other words, if there is genuine regard and compassion for the client by the therapist, and if the client believes in the therapist's belief in him or her, then healing can occur. Some call it unconditional positive regard, others call it presence. Some just call it love (that second-hand emotion).

The same is true for communities. *It is pain that brings you to the crossroads, but it is Love that pulls you through.* What else is there? It is the reason we endure the costs and stomach the sacrifices, so we can give to the people we love the values and things that we cherish. It is the reason we stay in the struggle when the going gets tough, rather than bail on the people we love. Knowing that we have been loved by God and by those in our life who have sacrificed for us, gives us the gratitude and obligation to love others and sacrifice for them in return.

To cooperate with grace means to risk loving again, and allowing ourselves to be loved again, when doubts and pain from old wounds would urge us to hold back. Cooperating with grace means learning to love, not in general, but specifically your community's members and its mission, as well as your God. The Journey of Transformation is not a concept or idea, it is an inside-out, soul-to-surface, wholly spiritual and concretely literal experience. It is love incarnate, love in action (John 15:12).

NEVER GO AHEAD OF GRACE

Our real journey in life is interior: it is a matter of growth, deepening, and of an ever greater surrender to the creative action of love and grace in our hearts.
Thomas Merton

Who will you be when all of your organizational changes are completed? Who are you becoming while you are making all your plans and getting things done? The Journey of Transformation takes seriously these questions. It invites you to explore the deeper invitations amid the multitude of changes communities are now facing. It invites you to discern God's call to new life.

The Sisters of St. Joseph have a maxim that says: "Never go ahead of grace by an impudent eagerness, but quietly await its movements, and, when it comes to you, go along with it with great gentleness, humility, fidelity, and courage."xv We ought not run ahead of grace, linger too long, or fall behind from where grace would want us to go or have us become. The Spirit moves in real time and blows where She will (John 3:8). We cannot engineer Her ways or control where She leads us. Only if we are attentive, courageous, nimble and disciplined enough, can we can learn to cooperate with grace.

Summary

We shall not cease from exploration, and the end of all our exploring will be to arrive where we started and know the place for the first time.
T. S. Eliot

The Journey of Transformation addresses a community's entire life and mission, not just the bricks and mortar of their lives. It engages and integrates the heart and soul of its members as they plan and co-create a vision for the future. It is multidimensional in that it addresses not only the organizational dimensions of community but also the personal and interpersonal dimensions. It is multilayered in that it goes beyond what you can see on the surface to also address the patterns, structures, worldview, and indeed the very culture and soul of community.

The Divine Mystery of transformation can partially be understood from our human perspective and the rest is left to mystery. Indeed, we need to understand what we can of this mystery, so that we know our part to play. We need to dispose ourselves to grace and learn how to cooperate with grace. The parts we can't see (grace of ambiguity) and can't control (grace of chaos) are integral to any faith journey. These underlying and unnerving aspects of a transformative journey require that a community grow in their capacity to use their instruments of faith (e.g., prayer, contemplation and discernment). Even so, at the end of all their planning, praying, organizing, discerning, implementing and evaluating, transformation will require them to take a leap of faith. The rest is grace.

Having now provided you with the origins, context, and foundational understandings for the Journey of Transformation and the inner work of transformation, let us move to the series of reflections. May these be an instrument for your personal an communal transformation.

PART III:
GRACED CROSSROADS

There's a thread you follow. It goes among things that change. But it doesn't change. People wonder about what you are pursuing. You have to explain about the thread. But it is hard for others to see. While you hold it you can't get lost. Tragedies happen; people get hurt or die; and you suffer and get old. Nothing you do can stop time's unfolding. You don't ever let go of the thread.
William Stafford. *The Way It Is*

GOD'S CALL, THE DEEPER INVITATION AND A JOURNEY OF FAITH

Throughout our lives, there is a thread we follow that resonates with our soul and beckons us to live and grow more fully into mature love and union with the Divine. I like to think of this thread as the movement of grace in our lives that continually summons our soul. If we follow the thread, and respond to the lure and love of God, our soul grows large in stature. We become wiser and more loving of one another, creation and our Creator. When we cooperate with grace in this way, we are more able to live out of a deep trust of God at work in our lives, and we live more authentically as our true selves.

THE INNER WORK OF TRANSFORMATION

As it turns out, however, following the thread is not so easy. Parker Palmer likens our soul to a wild animal, strong and resilient, on the one hand, but shy and reluctant to show itself in the face of threat, on the other hand. Our soul thrives in places where love abounds, but not in places where judgment, deceit or violence are experienced. It flourishes in response to the realness of life, even its rawness, but not amidst false perfumes, sugar coated pretense, gossip, or hostility. In places that are inhospitable to our soul, it is hard to follow the thread.

Assisting our shy but resilient soul in navigating our world is our ego. Some refer to this part of our being as our false self or worldly self. It might just as well be called the navigator because that is what it does. It helps us navigate life's realness and rawness along with its pretense and violence. Our navigator is more cunning and crafty than our soul, especially when it comes to the pretense and violence in our world. It has ways of exerting control and coping mechanisms of all kinds in order to: anticipate and avert danger, create safety and security, discriminate reality from illusion, as well as seek pleasure and minimize pain. The greater our capacity to navigate, the more able we are to find our way through the world.

You might think of your ego and the soul as being on the same team rather than adversaries, as some suggest. If the ego is the navigator, then you might think of the soul as its pilot. The pilot determines the destination and needs the navigator to tell you how to get there. Each part is necessary, serves a purpose, makes us human, makes us whole. We are one whole being, a mixture of flesh and spirit, ego and soul, made in the image of God. Most contemporary theologians would agree with Richard Rohr, who addresses this false dichotomy between our ego and soul this way: "It is not about becoming spiritual beings nearly as much as about becoming human beings…. That's why so much of the (bible) text seems so mundane, practical, specific and, frankly unspiritual!" "We have created a terrible kind of dualism between the spiritual (soul) and the so-called non-spiritual (ego). This dualism precisely is what Jesus came to reveal as a lie."

Thus, we are one whole being, both human and divine. The ego and the soul are ideally a team. They need each other and, like any team, sometimes they work well together and sometimes not. When they do not work well together, we are at risk. If our navigator exerts too much control, and our soul's desires are silenced, we are at risk of losing our self. If our soul's desires lure us into relationships, jobs or circumstances we cannot adequately navigate, we are also at risk. We need both to function well together.

As we develop and mature, we become more able to integrate this partnership and actualize our potential and bring fulness to our true self. The more integrated and harmonious the partnership between our ego and our soul becomes, the better able we are to follow the thread. Jesus followed the thread. He epitomized this harmonious integration between the ego and soul, between humanity and divinity. Gandhi, Martin Luther King, Dorothy Day and countless others have modeled this for us as well.

Hopefully you have had personal mentors in your own life who, along with your spiritual ancestors, have inspired you to integrate your soul and ego. Men and women such as these radiate wisdom, compassion, and unconditional love by the very way they walk among us and participate in God's unfolding dream. Psychologists call them fully actualized human beings. Our Church calls them mystics, saints or martyrs.

REFLECTION 1:
YOUR GRACED CROSSROADS

Thus says the Lord: "Stand by the roads, and look, and ask for the ancient paths, where the good way is; and walk in it, and find rest for your souls."
Jeremiah 6:16

When our life becomes separated from our soul

When our soul and our ego are at odds and unintegrated, we can easily lose our bearings and our grasp of the thread. When our life becomes separated from our soul in this way, things start to unravel. We can start to chase after grace, lag behind it, or try to control it in an effort to bend life toward our predilections. We can lose a sense of being grounded in reality, what is right and true. We are at risk of falling apart and losing our true self. When the partnership between our soul and ego breaks down, we break down.

This breakdown and loss of self can happen so easily, often gradually and imperceptibly over time, until a tipping point is reached. Sometimes, our work becomes so important that we get lost in it. At other times, because of our fear of losing an important relationship, we compromise our true self to the point where we lose our voice, our opinions, our power and eventually our self. The opposite also happens. Out of a fear of losing our independence, or because we were shamed into thinking we are unlovable, we hide and live out of a false persona. We become imposters, appearing strong and independent, fending off any hint of dependency or our desire for intimate connections with others, lost to our true self.

Despite our best efforts, we can lose ourselves in just about anything: hobbies, work, television, social media, addictions, and relationships, even in our efforts to become more holy. When this happens, it is as if the ground beneath us has shifted and the bottom has fallen out. Our best-laid plans for assembling our life as we wish it to be (e.g., secure, pleasurable, predictable and controlled), are foiled. We reach a point where nothing makes sense anymore. We drift from our soul and lose our grasp of the thread. Our ego and our soul are in turmoil. Our constructed world and false personas crumble, and we are beset with dread and despair.

These are the times in our life that either make us or break us. We either evolve into a more mature way of being or we devolve and crumble. These are "come-to-Jesus" moments wherein we either face the deeper truths that we have otherwise kept hidden under the floorboards of consciousness, or we press harder to deny them and fall more deeply into slumber (Romans 13:11). We either reclaim, renew and expand our soul, becoming more fully who we are meant to be, or our spirit capitulates and our soul shrivels. We might rail against such predicaments, but none of our protestations will lift us from the hole we have dug for ourselves. There is no way out of such crises other than through them. We are at a crossroads and forced to choose.

Amidst all of our groaning, there is, at the same time, a quiet voice whispering, inviting us to choose life. We stand at the threshold of either our own demise or our own freedom. But we do not stand there alone. God is with us at the crossroads, just as in every nook and cranny of creation. "Where can I go from your Spirit? Where can I flee from your presence? If I go up to the heavens, you are there; if I make my bed in the depths, you are there. If I rise on the wings of the dawn, if I settle on the far side of the sea, even there your hand will guide me, your right hand will hold me fast." (Psalm 139:7-10)

We are at a *graced crossroads* because God is with us. The thread we had tried to follow, and thought we had somehow lost, while just beyond our grasp, is well within our reach. We have only to reach for it. To choose life will mean relying less on our own reason or egoic machinations, and more on discerning our soul's desire.

There are no shortcuts or guarantees. There is no map or formula. To choose life at a graced crossroads is always a leap of faith requiring a renewed covenant of cooperation with grace. There are endless ways we can lose our self, but there is only one way home, unique to each of us. Our soul knows its way. We have only to let go of the reins, our illusions of control, and act with courage. We have only to listen for the beckoning love of God as our guide through the graced crossroads.

MEDITATIONS

Rumi

See how the hand is invisible while the pen is writing; the horse careening, yet the rider unseen; the arrow flying, but the bow out of sight; individual souls existing, while the Soul of souls is hidden.

1 Corinthians 15:10

For I am the least of the apostles, and not fit to be called an apostle, because I persecuted the church of God. But by the grace of God I am what I am, and His grace toward me did not prove vain; but I labored even more than all of them, yet not I, but the grace of God within me.

Francis Thompson. The Hound of Heaven

I fled Him, down the nights and down the days;
I fled Him, down the arches of the years;
I fled Him, down the labyrinthine ways
Of my own mind; and in the mist of tears
I hid from Him, and under running laughter.
Up vistaed hopes I sped;
And shot, precipitated,
Adown Titanic glooms of chasmed fears,

From those strong Feet that followed,
Followed after.
But with unhurrying chase
And unperturbed pace
Deliberate speed, majestic instancy,
They beat – and a Voice beat
More instant than the Feet –
'All things betray thee,
Who betrayest Me.'

JOURNAL REFLECTIONS AND EXERCISES

Wake up! Your life is about to change

Recall one of your own crossroads from the past. Recall an occasion in your life through which, driven by a painful awareness of your own brokenness and simultaneously lured by grace, you fell apart, were transformed and became new again. These are typically occasions in life in which you experienced the most pain and, by your own cooperation with grace, you experienced the most growth. These may have been sparked by a sudden event (e.g., an illness, a failure in pursuit of a dream, a loss of someone or something you loved) or a gradual and gnawing awareness that something wasn't quite right anymore.

In either case, you reached a point where you became painfully aware that the life you were living was no longer the life you were meant to live. The life you were living no longer represented your true self, your deeper calling. You became separated from the thread, the moorings of your soul, and the pain of this separation became unbearable. You had reached a graced crossroads in which the choices you would make would forever change your life.

1. Give it a headline. Think back across your life's journey and recall one of your own graced crossroads. Or maybe you are at such a crossroads at the present time. In either case, jot down a headline (a sentence or two) that captures what your graced crossroads holds for you. Give your story a title.

Now dwell upon your graced crossroads. Bring back these memories through journaling, sharing with a confidant, rummaging through keepsakes or going back to the physical location where this experience occurred. Recall what was happening in your life during this period of time. Recall where you were living and with whom, where you were employed or ministering. Think back on what had been working that eventually became untenable. Call to mind what brought you to live the life you had been living before you reached a crossroads. Immerse yourself in these memories, thoughts and feelings, and describe your full experience. Write the story you remember.

1. Describe the original dream. Describe the dream you had once pursued before things fell apart (e.g., someone or something you loved and sought to pursue). Recall, also, the passion you once felt, and the leap of faith you once took, in order to pursue that original dream. What were the life-giving reasons you had for choosing that original dream? What secret motivations might you also have had in making that choice (i.e., things you may not have wanted to admit to yourself or others, or maybe only now realize in retrospect)?

2. Describe why things fell apart. Reflect on why things fell apart and why you fell apart. There may have been circumstances and events outside of you that brought you to your knees, but focus here more upon your own choices. Explore the repetitive patterns or specific choices you made that chipped away at that original dream and foreclosed on the life you were living. For example:

   a. Perhaps you made choices born of naivete or insecurity. In what ways were you naïve or immature and how did this play out in the life you were living?

   b. Maybe it was your benign neglect or not dealing with things you knew should have been addressed at the time. How do you understand your neglect or avoidance of things that mattered?

   c. Perhaps a part of you wanted things to fall apart and bring it all to an end. Did you intentionally sabotage efforts to repair things in order to say to yourself, "See, it isn't working anymore!"

d. Maybe unredeemed wounds from your past may have caused you to act out and make choices driven by fear, anger, shame, jealousy or some other unbridled emotion. What were those wounds of the past?

e. Perhaps you were growing, making choices more in line with who you were becoming, choices no longer nourishing or compatible with your former dream. What new parts of yourself were emerging?

Identify at least three specific reasons (choices you made or patterns you exhibited) that led to your life unraveling.

3. Describe your fall. Recall how your life had become increasingly out of alignment and at odds with your soul. Recall the signs early on that things were no longer working. You may have been conscious of these at the time or only now in retrospect. At the worst of it, when things were completely unraveling and you were hitting bottom, what were you experiencing physically, emotionally and spiritually? Recall the terror, shame, rage and utter vulnerability you may have experienced.

WISDOM FROM THE PAST, APPLIED TO THE PRESENT

Having reflected upon a past personal experience of transformation, gather the insights and learnings and apply it to the present. If your community is currently engaged in the work of transformation, answer the same four sets of reflection questions from the perspective of the community as a whole. If you are currently going through your own personal transformation, answer the same reflection questions as applied to you today.

Communal transformation

1. Offer a headline that captures your community's work of transformation.

2. Describe the community's original dream.

3. Identify why you think your community is falling apart.

4. Describe the experience of your community's falling apart.

Personal transformation

1. Offer a headline that captures your personal experience of transformation.

2. Describe your original dream.

3. Identify why you are falling apart.

4. Describe the experience of your falling apart.

REFLECTION 2:
THE DEEPER INVITATION

You are what your deep, driving desire is.
As your desire is, so is your will.
As your will is, so is your deed.
As your deed is, so is your destiny.
Brihadaranyaka Upanishad

GOD'S CALL TO CHOOSE LIFE

When our life is falling apart, and we are approaching a crisis, our typical response is to ramp up our efforts to try harder, rather than to try differently. We become increasingly desperate in our attempts to control the situation, and restore what was, by doing more of what worked in the past. But when we reach a crossroads, and Humpty Dumpty can't be put together again, we realize that we can't go back to the way things were. When we can no longer fix things, and when the pain finally overwhelms us, we break down. If our break-down is severe enough, if we completely unravel, we hit, as they say, "bottom."

When we hit bottom, we are stripped from any hubris that we can solve things on our own. While the experience is excruciating, we are finally liberated from the chains of the past, the prisons of our own making and from our failed attempts to repair things on our own. We are stripped of our defenses, our pretense and our ability to hide our brokenness. Our life is laid bare for all to see. We are finally open to receive what we have repeatedly rebuffed, to take the risks we have continually sidestepped, and to listen to our soul's response to a deeper invitation that we have previously failed to hear: "Take My yoke upon you and learn from Me, for I am gentle and humble in heart, and you will find rest for your souls. For My yoke is easy and My burden is light" (Matthew 11:29-30).

While hitting bottom is agonizing, there is also a strange peace amidst the storm, much like the eye of a hurricane. Finally, we can stop trying so hard, and we can let go of our desperation. It's not working. Finally, we can lay down the illusion and the burden that we alone are in control of things. Clearly, we are not. At last, we can stop agonizing over what to do. Obviously, we don't know and can no longer navigate things on our own. We know that we need help. It's undeniable to ourselves, even if we can't yet speak it aloud to others. We know deep down inside that something is at work that is more profound and powerful than our own illusions of control and independence, even if we can't describe it. We simply know, from this point forward, that life will never be the same.

There is a difference between restoring things back to the way they were versus becoming new again. There is a difference between fashioning a "new and improved" version of ourselves versus transforming ourselves. When our lives are laid bare like this, we have a choice: take the well-worn path of least resistance or take the path less traveled and evolve into something altogether new. It is at these graced crossroads in our life, amidst the peaceful quietude of mature surrender, that the still small voice is heard, "Choose life." We wonder: *What does this mean? What is the deeper invitation and what does grace have to do with it?*

MEDITATIONS

Charlie Badenhop. Pure Heart, Simple Mind

We all need to decide whether to "play it safe" in life and worry about the down-side, or instead take a chance, by being who we really are and living the life our heart desires. Which choice are you making?

1 Kings 19:11-13

Then He said, "Go out, and stand on the mountain before the Lord." And behold, the Lord passed by, and a great and strong wind tore into the mountains and broke the rocks in pieces before the Lord, but the Lord was not in the wind; and after the wind an earthquake, but the Lord was not in the earthquake; and after the earthquake a fire, but the Lord was not in the fire; and after the fire a still small voice.

Deuteronomy 30:18-20

I declare to you today that you shall surely perish. You will not prolong your days in the land where you are crossing the Jordan to enter and possess it. I call heaven and earth to witness against you today, that I have set before you life and death, the blessing and the curse. So choose life in order that you may live, you and your descendants, by loving the LORD your God, by obeying His voice, and by holding fast to Him; for this is your life and the length of your days, that you may live in the land which the LORD swore to your fathers, to Abraham, Isaac, and Jacob, to give them.

Nan C. Merrill. Psalms for Praying: An Invitation to Wholeness

Though a thousand may deride this radical trust,
ten thousand laugh as I seek to do your will,
yet will I surrender myself to You,
abandoning myself into your hands without reserve.

Journal Reflections and Exercises

Reflect further upon the specific graced crossroads you identified at the beginning of this section.

1. Describe the deeper invitation. Recall any stirrings you may have experienced to "choose life." Despite the pain you were experiencing, what was stirring deep within you that may have given you a sense of security or hope, however vague or tenuous? Did you recognize that still small voice (1 Kings 19:11-13)? Whose voice was it and what was it trying to say to you? In what ways, if at all, did you experience the lure and love of God or the movements of grace during this time? Describe how you understood these stirrings from within and why you chose to listen.

2. Describe what you needed to let go, or let die, in order to respond to this deeper invitation. In other words, what jobs, person(s), commitments, possessions or pursuits did you ultimately choose to leave behind in order to make way for something or someone new? What personal or interpersonal habit patterns did you choose to lay down in favor of a new way of being? What core beliefs were shattered and what shifted in your soul?

3. Describe how you chose to nourish this deeper invitation. Recall the new life possibilities you were being called to consider. Recall the seeds of new life that were aching to be born. Describe the choices you made to deliberately nourish and bring these to life.

Wisdom from the past, applied to the present

Having reflected upon a past personal experience of transformation, gather the insights and learnings and apply it to the present. If your community is currently engaged in the work of transformation, answer the same reflection questions from the perspective of the community as a whole. If you are currently going through your own personal transformation, answer the same reflection questions as applied to you today.

Communal transformation

1. Describe what might be the deeper invitation for your community at this time.

2. Describe what your community needs to let go, or let die, in order to respond to this deeper invitation.

3. Describe how your community might nourish this deeper invitation.

Personal transformation

1. Describe what might be a deeper invitation for you at this time.

2. Describe what you needed to let go, or let die, in order to respond to this deeper invitation.

3. Describe how you might choose to nourish this deeper invitation.

REFLECTION 3:
A HIDDEN WHOLENESS

There is in all things… a hidden wholeness.
Thomas Merton

FALLING INTO GRACE

When we fall apart and hit bottom, it is not really a fall from grace, as is often said. It might be better to think of it as *falling into grace.* And when we fall into grace, we have an opportunity to experience what Merton described as a "hidden wholeness." In that hidden wholeness we are transfixed and transformed. We are brought to a new consciousness, a new level of awareness, a new presence. It is what the mystics regularly experience, but what most of us only rarely experience.

What is that wholeness that is beyond our ordinary awareness? For Merton, it is wisdom. The wisdom about which Merton speaks is not what we find by Googling. It is wisdom that comes from our lives encountering God, our direct experience of the Divine, the Holy Spirit or Risen Christ.

Some call this hidden wholeness beauty. But is not the surface beauty we see through our ordinary eyesight. It is the Beauty seen as God's sees. Seeing in this way, through the gaze of God, we become the person each one of us truly is. For others its name is love or truth. Hidden wholeness is a love that is God's Love. It is a truth that is God's Truth. We may not even know what we are experiencing, or how to name it, but it is there all the same, all around us.

There is in all things an invisible fecundity. It is not only all around us, but it is also within us, in all of our physical senses and in every cell of our being. We share it with God. The wholeness of our being is drenched in the wholeness of God. It is animated in all things. Our lives are the hidden wholeness enveloped by the wholeness of God. If we dispose ourselves to see and embrace it, then we can not only experience it ourselves, but we can also make it visible and accessible to the world.

In a recent gathering I facilitated, one of the participants thought of the hidden wholeness this way. "The Big Bang," she said, "was a big buildup of God's Love exploding with such force it became matter. We are made of stardust, particles of God's love." In other words, implanted in every particle of the universe is God's love. Therefore, God is in us as we are in God. If only we could make that more visible and accessible to the world!

This wisdom, beauty, love, truth or whatever name you give it, is hidden by our brokenness, just as it is hidden in our brokenness. It is hidden by our humanity, just as it is hidden in our humanity. It is hidden by the shadow of death and in the shadow of death. There, in all of these hidden places, is tenderness, mercy, and compassion.

It is beyond all words. Each one of us, and every faith tradition, tries to attach words to this ineffable hidden wholeness: Wisdom, Beauty, Love, Light, Mercy, Compassion, Goodness, Sweetness, Jesus Christ, the Risen Christ, the Holy Spirit, or God. None of them are adequate, but all of them are rich with meaning, nuance, and depth. Living in this hidden wholeness means living in the fullness and aliveness of the Mystery of God. In this we are consoled and transformed. We are brought to a new consciousness. We are made new again. We see the hidden wholeness of others. If only we could see each other that way all the time!

MEDITATIONS

Thomas Merton. Hagia Sophia

There is in all visible things an invisible fecundity, a dimmed light, a meek name-lessness, a hidden wholeness. This mysterious Unity and Integrity is Wisdom, the Mother of all, Natura naturans. There is in all things an inexhaustible sweetness and purity, a silence that is a fount of action and joy. It rises up in wordless gentle-ness and flows out to me from the unseen roots of all created being, welcoming me tenderly, saluting me with indescribable humility. This is at once my own being, my own nature, and the Gift of my Creator's Thought and Art within me, speaking as Hagia Sophia, speaking as my sister, Wisdom.

Thomas Merton. Conjectures of a Guilty Bystander

In Louisville, at the corner of Fourth and Walnut, in the center of the shop-ping district, I was suddenly overwhelmed with the realization that I loved all these people, that they were mine and I theirs, that we could not be alien to one another even though we were total strangers. It was like waking from a dream of separateness, of spurious self-isolation in a special world. . . .

Then it was as if I suddenly saw the secret beauty of their hearts, the depths of their hearts where neither sin nor desire nor self-knowledge can reach, the core of their reality, the person that each one is in God's eyes. If only they could all see themselves as they really are. If only we could see each other that way all the time. There would be no more war, no more hatred, no more cruelty, no more greed. . . . But this cannot be seen, only believed and 'understood' by a peculiar gift.

JOURNAL REFLECTIONS AND EXERCISES

Go back to your crossroads experience. Recall what it was like for you to journey through a transformation from life, through death, to new life again.

1. When you hit bottom and fell into grace, what treasures previ-ously hidden, ultimately were revealed to you?

2. What was the new life flowing out of the Hidden Wholeness?

Wisdom from the past, applied to the present

Having reflected upon a past personal experience of transformation, gather the insights and learnings and apply it to the present. If your community is currently engaged in the work of transformation, answer the same reflection questions from the perspective of the community as a whole. If you are currently going through your own personal transformation, answer the same reflection questions as applied to you today.

Communal transformation

1. As your community falls into grace, what treasures previously hidden, might be revealed?

2. What might be the new life to which your community is being called, flowing out of the Hidden Wholeness?

Personal transformation

1. As you experience falling into grace, what treasures previously hidden, might be revealed?

2. What might be the new life to which you are being called, flowing out of the Hidden Wholeness?

Reflection 4:
The Narrow Gate

Enter through the narrow gate; for the gate is wide and the way is broad that leads to destruction, and there are many who enter through it. For the gate is small and the way is narrow that leads to life, and there are few who find it.
Matthew 7:13-14

Choosing the right way over the easy way

I don't know why God set it up this way, why fear has such a dominant role in the choices we make in life, but it does. Perhaps that's why the bible has over 350 references to fear and how, with God's help, we can overcome it.

Don't put your foot in the bucket!

I'll never forget hearing my Dad's voice from behind home plate, while playing in my first Little League baseball game. "Don't put your foot in the bucket! Stay down on the ball!" At the age of seven, I didn't know exactly what he meant by the bucket, but I knew a lot about fear, and I knew I was backing away from the baseball being hurled in my direction.

After the game, I recall sitting, head slumped, while crying in the front seat of the car with my father. He explained that the batter's box is the white rectangular shaped box in which the batter stands when ready for the pitch. When you "put your foot in the bucket," he said, "it means you stepped out of the batter's box." I cried, ashamed that I was so afraid of being hit by the ball. I had put my foot in the bucket over and over again. I wept because I disappointed my father who loved baseball and wanted his son to love it too.

It was a painful life-lesson and also one of the most tender memories I have of my father. He wasn't admonishing me. He had his arm around me, consoling me, teaching me about fear, and encouraging me not to back away in the face of it. He was loving me, even in my shame. I have felt his arm around me my entire life as I continue to face my fears.

The narrow gate

The narrow gate for me represents stepping up to the plate and doing what's right, not what is safe or easy. It is the narrow path that leads to life, while the path most often traveled leads to death and destruction. The wider path that most will travel is the path of least resistance. It costs little (on the front end) and is familiar, predictable and safe. It seems safe, when, in fact, it is the riskiest of all because it takes us away from where grace is inviting us to go. We choose it out of fear and it limits us. It silences our soul.

Again, I don't know why God set it up this way, but the way to new life means having the courage to walk through the narrow gate. The way to growth, the way to wisdom, requires facing our fears without putting our foot in bucket. The inner work of transformation means mustering the courage to risk whatever pain we might encounter, out of a deep trust that God's arm is still around us, encouraging us, consoling us and inviting us to choose life.

MEDITATIONS

Robert Frost. The Road Not Taken

Two roads diverged in a yellow wood, and sorry I could not travel both, and be one traveler, long I stood, and looked down one as far as I could, to where it bent in the undergrowth;

Then took the other, as just as fair, and having perhaps the better claim, because it was grassy and wanted wear, though as for that the passing there, had worn them really about the same,

And both that morning equally lay in leaves no step had trodden black. Oh, I kept the first for another day! Yet knowing how way leads on to way I doubted if I should ever come back.

I shall be telling this with a sigh somewhere ages and ages hence: Two roads diverged in a wood, and I, I took the one less traveled by, and that has made all the difference.

Psalm 23:3-5

He restores my soul; He guides me in the paths of righteousness for His name's sake. Even though I walk through the valley of the shadow of death, I fear no evil, for You are with me; Your rod and Your staff, they comfort me. You prepare a table before me in the presence of my enemies; You have anointed my head with oil; My cup overflows.

M. Scott Peck. The Road Less Traveled: A New Psychology of Love, Traditional Values, and Spiritual Growth

Human beings are poor examiners, subject to superstition, bias, prejudice, and a profound tendency to see what they want to see rather than what is really there.

Margaret Blackie. Give Us This Day, Grace to Weather the Storm

What are we to do when storms threaten to tear apart the very fabric of our lives? All I can say with certainty is that Jesus is not asleep. He is paying attention, but the storms rarely get resolved quite so simply. I pray for the storm to pass. I pray for the grace to weather the storm.

Praying for the grace is a shorthand term to describe a process I have learned to use. It begins with acknowledging the presence of the storm. Then I find it helpful to focus on Jesus' question: Why are you afraid? I begin to mentally explore the situation, to ask myself what I dread or what is paralyzing me. Then I ask for the grace to be released from that fear.

In a world that actively generates fear, we often forget that fear is profoundly problematic. It is probably the greatest barrier to our transformation. We cannot move forward in faith until we have learned how to sit with our fear, to recognize it, to name it, and pray for the grace to be released from it.

We think our faith will be cemented when we are rescued from our storms. In the long term, our faith is best served by learning to navigate our difficulties in conversation with Jesus. Engaging with the tough questions – why are you afraid?

If we dare to start asking those questions, we begin to discover that true freedom is not a mythical place beyond the reach of trials, tribulations, and tragedies. Rather, it comes when we are able to navigate our way through these things without being capsized. True freedom takes us to a place where we can suffer terrible losses without totally losing ourselves or losing companionship with God.

JOURNAL REFLECTIONS AND EXERCISES

Go back to your crossroads experience. Recall the fear and other disconcerting emotions you may have felt at that graced crossroads:

1. Explore the purpose of this narrow gate. Why do you think God has set it up this way, that the path to new life frightens us so much? Why is it that the narrow gate and road less traveled is the way to God, while the wider gate and well-trodden path leads us away from God?

2. Recall those times when you put your foot in the bucket. In what ways did you shy away from stepping up to the plate? When did fear win out over courage? Explore why this happened, how you felt about it, and where that led you.

3. Identify what eventually gave you the courage to go through the narrow gate. When did your courage finally win out over fear? Reflect upon what it cost you and what you gained. Who, in your life, has helped you to stay in the batter's box, consoling you, holding you and encouraging you along the way?

WISDOM FROM THE PAST, APPLIED TO THE PRESENT

Having reflected upon a past personal experience of transformation, gather the insights and learnings and apply it to the present. If your community is currently engaged in the work of transformation, answer the same reflection questions from the perspective of the community as a whole. If you are currently going through your own personal transformation, answer the same reflection questions as applied to you today.

Communal transformation

1. Explore the purpose of this narrow gate for your community at this time.

2. Recall those times when your community put its collective foot in the bucket.

3. Identify what is giving your community the courage to go through the narrow gate.

Personal transformation

1. Explore the purpose of this narrow gate for you at this time.

2. Explore when and how you might be putting your foot in the bucket.

3. Reflect upon what might give you the courage to go through the narrow gate today.

REFLECTION 5:
A MYSTERY KNOWN
BY FAITH

When you get to the end of all the light you know and it's time to step into the darkness of the unknown, faith is knowing that one of two things shall happen: either you will be given something solid to stand on, or you will be taught how to fly.
Edward Teller

COOPERATION WITH GRACE

The rub in the Paschal Mystery is that God's gift of new life comes only after our dying, not before. We have to let die what needs to die in order for new life to emerge, and we can't know ahead of time what this new life will be. This Divine gift of newness surpasses all human understanding, foreknowledge or control. It is ultimately and always a leap of faith. Such is the way of deep change that we, as Christians, call the Paschal Mystery.

That we can't engineer or guarantee the outcome, or that we cannot know ahead of time what will emerge from this leap of faith, in no way implies that we are completely blind or have nothing to do with its unfolding. While these life-death-new-life transformations are mysterious, the mystery is not a black abyss of complete unknowns. We have learned some things about the nature of transformation through contemporary science and humanities. We have also gleaned some knowledge though our lived experience of transformation. Most importantly, the mystery of transformation is the Mystery known to us by our faith. If we have lived a life of faith, we have some experience we can draw upon that will give us our bearings.

While the terrain at a graced crossroads may be new and uncharted, the landscape darker than in more stable times, we have a compass and lantern to guide our way. Our compass points are the faith experiences we have come to know throughout our lives. We know, for example, what *truth* is when we experience it. We know what *mercy* is when we receive it. We know what genuine *reconciliation* requires of us. We know when we are being *honest* and when we are not. These are not mysteries. These are powerful spiritual touchstones. This soul-knowledge may be beyond reason and hard to prove to others; we know it when we experience it. These compass points or touchstones have been etched into our soul, are unique to each one of us, and spring from the basement of time.

The "dark night," as St. John of the Cross described it, is dark for a reason. He taught us that God has to work under the cover of darkness and in secret because, if we fully knew what was happening, and what grace will eventually ask of us, we would either try to change or stop the whole process. Still the dark night is not pitch black. The lantern we have, though not as luminous as we'd like, gives us more than enough light once we let our eyes adjust.

We can see with the eyesight of faith in much of this darkness. Our lantern is illumed by our instruments of faith: prayer, discernment and contemplation. With these tools, we can see, feel and discern our way through the subtleties of light and dark. Through prayer and reflection, we can sift and sort what is right and true, what would bring a smile to God's face, and what is of our own making that might lead us astray. With our compass and our lantern to light our way we can follow the thread, cooperate with grace and do our part to pursue the "new."

An additional way we can cooperate with grace is through our choices of mature surrender, a deliberate choice to let go of someone or something we love in order to give life to something new. Mature surrender is different than throwing in the towel or capitulation because we see ourselves as victims of circumstances and as having no choice. It is not a letting go because we have no will of our own (throwing up our hands and, saying, "It's God's will").

It takes a certain maturity in order to intentionally choose by our own free will the pain of letting go so that something new might be born. Furthermore, it takes a certain amount of maturity to freely let go of someone or something we love while not knowing for sure if new life will emerge or exactly what it might be if it does. Making these choices of our own free will, while not having the control or foreknowledge we might otherwise prefer, takes a great deal of courage and maturity.

MEDITATIONS

Rumi

Without cause God gave us Being; without cause give it back again. Gambling yourself away is beyond any religion. Religion seeks grace and favor, but those who gamble these away are God's favorites, for they neither put God to the test nor knock at the door of gain and loss.

Ken Kesey

The answer is never the answer. What's really interesting is the mystery. If you seek the mystery instead of the answer, you'll always be seeking. I've never seen anybody really find the answer. They think they have, so they stop thinking. But the job is to seek mystery, evoke mystery, plant a garden in which strange plants grow and mysteries bloom. The need for mystery is greater than the need for an answer.

John 3:1-21

Now there was a Pharisee, a man named Nicodemus who was a member of the Jewish ruling council. He came to Jesus at night and said, "Rabbi, we know that you are a teacher who has come from God. For no one could perform the signs you are doing if God were not with him." Jesus replied, "Very truly I tell you, no one can see the kingdom of God unless they are born again." "How can someone be born when they are old?" Nicodemus asked. "Surely they cannot enter a second time into their mother's womb to be born!" Jesus answered, "Very truly I tell you, no one can enter the kingdom of God unless they are born of water and the Spirit. Flesh gives birth to flesh, but the Spirit gives birth to spirit. You should not be surprised at my saying, 'You must be born again.' The wind blows wherever it pleases. You hear its sound, but you cannot tell where it comes from or where it is going. So it is with everyone born of the Spirit."

Psalm 119:105-107

Your word is a lamp for my feet and a light for my path. I took an oath, and I will keep it. I took an oath to follow your regulations, which are based on your righteousness. I have suffered so much. Give me a new life, O Lord, as you promised.

Richard Rohr. Daily Meditation

In the moments of insecurity and crisis, "shoulds" and "oughts" don't really help; they just increase the shame, guilt, pressure, and likelihood of backsliding. It's the deep "yeses" that carry you through. Focusing on something you absolutely believe in, that you're committed to, will help you wait it out.

JOURNAL REFLECTIONS AND EXERCISES

Go back to your crossroads experience. Recall what it was like for you to journey through a transformation from life, to death, to new life again.

1. Identify your compass points. When you journeyed through a "dark night" of your own soul, what familiar compass points gave you the assurance that you were on the path of faith? What spiritual touchstones informed and validated your choices, telling you that you were on the right path, a path that was leading you to new life?

2. Explore what it means for you to cooperate with grace. How did you know or intuit when you had a hold of the thread, that you

were actually cooperating with grace? What did it feel like? What did you do, concretely and specifically, in order to cooperate with grace? How did you know that you were not resisting, running ahead, lagging behind, or trying to control grace?

3. Recall a choice you made for mature surrender and the comfort that may have come from it. You likely made some of these deliberate painful choices to let go, knowing these were necessary in order to make room for the possibility of new life. What were some of your own mature surrenderings? How was that different than throwing in the towel? What gave you comfort in the midst of all the ambiguity to live through the pain of letting go?

WISDOM FROM THE PAST, APPLIED TO THE PRESENT

Having reflected upon a past personal experience of transformation, gather the insights and learnings and apply it to the present. If your community is currently engaged in the work of transformation, answer the same reflection questions from the perspective of the community as a whole. If you are currently going through your own personal transformation, answer the same reflection questions as applied to you today.

Communal transformation

1. Identify your community's compass points.

2. Explore the ways in which your community is cooperating with grace.

3. Reflect upon the choices your community is making for mature surrender.

Personal transformation

1. Identify your personal compass points.

2. Explore the ways in which you are cooperating with grace.

3. Reflect upon the choices you are making for mature surrender.

PART IV:
DYNAMIC ELEMENTS
OF TRANSFORMATION

The real truth, I have come to think, is that there is no such thing as having only one life to live. The fact is that every life is simply a series of lives, each one of them with its own task, its own flavor, its own brand of efforts, its own type of sins, its own glories, its own kind of deep, dank despair, its own plethora of possibilities, all designed to lead us to the same end – happiness and a sense of fulfillment.

Most apparent to me now is that each of our separate lives, however much they are part of one continuous lifeline, is discrete. Each of them is distinct, is actually a uniquely apprehensible part of the whole of life. Each of them makes us new. And each of them has a purpose.
Joan Chittister. The Gift of Years

TRANSFORMATION AS THE PASCHAL MYSTERY

The Journey of Transformation, while encompassing deep personal, communal and systemic change is, in essence, a journey of faith. While much of what we know of transformation remains a mystery, we are growing familiar with its ways. You have begun to explore some of these ways in Parts I, II and III. You have reflected upon what brings you to these crossroads, the deeper invitations at the crossroads, a hidden wholeness, what is asked of you in order to pass through the narrow gate, and what it means to cooperate with grace. What else do we know of this faith journey and the soulwork required of us along the way?

Recall, once again, the graced crossroads experience you identified in Part III. When you were transformed, every part of your being was changed – your values, identity, primary commitments, your purpose in life, and your relationship with God. As we move through transformative experiences in life, our soul, psyche and relational webs all evolve. Incorporating who we were before this transformation took place, we ultimately transcend who we once were and literally become new again, "Truly, truly, I say to you, unless one is born again he cannot see the kingdom of God" (John 3:3).

What are the psycho-social-spiritual elements involved when we go through such deep changes in our lives? In part II, I briefly introduced you to the five dynamic elements that are intrinsic to this soulwork. These elements are dynamic in that they interact and are interconnected. These are not separate, discrete, linear steps taken one at a time but organically interwoven throughout the Journey of Transformation. We might focus our attention on one or another of these at a given point in time, but each is part of the whole spiraling movement. As you work your way through the spiral, you are engaged repeatedly in ever-deepening ways with all five of these dynamic elements.

These five dynamic elements comprise the essence of the inner work of transformation. These are the personal and interpersonal ways of cooperating with grace. These elements are present whether we speak of *conversion* from a spiritual perspective, *healing* from a psycho-social perspective or *systemic change* from an organizational perspective. These are the elements woven into all three levels involved in communal transformation: personal (emotional and spiritual), interpersonal (relational and communal) and systemic (structural and organizational).

The purpose of Part IV is to help you understand and work with these five dynamic elements from your own personal experience rather than from an abstract, theoretical perspective. If you can understand how these elements have been part of your own transformative experiences, then you might feel a bit more comfortable and confident as you live through the inherent chaos of transformation that you and your community may be experiencing. Understanding these elements will give you some hooks around which you can attach your experience throughout the journey of personal and communal transformation. Working with these reflections will provide you with a means for cooperating with grace in your own journey of transformation.

FIVE DYNAMIC ELEMENTS

While I introduced these five elements in Part II, let me review these once again for your work here in Part IV. In this review I will describe the role of each element as it pertains to both personal and communal transformation. Following this introduction, you will be invited to reflect upon each of these elements according to the transformative experiences you identified in Part III. You will then be invited to gather the wisdom from the past and use it to better understand and engage in your community's journey of transformation. Additionally, if you are currently at a crossroads in your own life, you will be invited to apply these past learnings to your personal journey of transformation.

1. Shifts in consciousness: creating a new narrative

Einstein famously taught us that we cannot solve today's problems with the same level of consciousness that gave rise to them. Healers have always known this as they emphasize the need to shift the perspectives, patterns, emotions and beliefs in which our wounds are embedded. Ultimately, a shift in perspective or a transformation of consciousness enables us to write a new narrative for our lives, one that is authentic, liberating and life-enhancing. It is this experience of pouring new wine into new wineskins that enables new life to emerge.

This is as important for individual transformation as it is for communal transformation. In other words, the community, as a whole, will need to make the same kind of shift. This involves a collective shift in the communal perspective regarding the meaning and purpose of your lives, reframing what mission and community mean to you, and rewriting the narrative of your communal faith journey.

Beyond a shift in perspective, though, there is the deeper work of growing toward higher levels of consciousness. For individuals and communities this requires practicing mindfulness in order to awaken and expand your personal and collective consciousness. Without this shift, or a deeper transformation of consciousness, you will see and, therefore, shape the future much as you have in the past. A new consciousness helps you to recognize the stories you are telling yourself that are no longer true and to open up new narratives that are more fitting with who you are becoming.

2. Reclaiming our inner voice: the seat and source of everything that lives

When we are broken, brought to our knees and have drifted from our own soul's desires, we eventually reach a point where this is no longer tenable. Our false self crumbles in the face of hypocrisy and we know our lives to be inauthentic. We start the long road back to reclaiming our true selves. We have to reclaim and re-authenticate our inner voice, renew our soul and retrieve our life in a whole new way. It is an heroic journey that brings us home to our true selves, to those we love, and to God.

The inner work of transformation requires that we recenter our soul within the stream of grace flowing through our lives. It is about having honest conversations with God and shedding the pretenses of our false self and the ego attachments that may have built up over time. In order for this to happen, we need to reclaim our true self and live more in alignment with our inner voice rather than live according to the expectations of others. We need to connect our soul to our life's purpose in today's world by discovering our innermost truths and authentic calling.

For communities this means taking off your masks and defensive armor in order to engage in highly intimate conversations about your deepest longings. This requires rebuilding trust and restoring the green space for growth to occur inside community (not just going outside community to grow). It means going through the dark night as a community in order to become more real and honest. It is a journey for heroic communities willing to reclaim their soul, the seat and source of their existence. Without this soulwork, without tapping their authentic inner voice, communities will merely change what is on the surface of their lives and build a house of cards as their vision for the future.

3. Reconciliation and conversion: the womb of our becoming

Reconciliation and conversion are essential for transformation to occur. This soulwork is the crucible of transformation. This is where change happens and "new" is born. We are converted when we are broken open and when we allow both pain and compassion to transforms us. This requires that we work through conflicts and address the issues we have otherwise avoided, or not successfully worked through, in order to break open and heal our wounds. This inner work is the womb of our becoming. It is where new is born.

Communities, like families, accumulate baggage, years of unresolved wounds and conflicts. Working through these conflicts, reconciling relationships, and healing the wounds of community is the heart-work of transformation. It is also the Achilles' heel for communities as most will not succeed without proper training and assistance. It is the kind of painful and messy personal and interpersonal work which most communities prefer to avoid. Without this work of reconciliation and conversion, though, there will be no transformation. Members will become more emotionally distanced and the collective whole will become increasingly fragmented.

4. Experimentation and learning: acting our way into a new way of being

In order to move through deep change, you will need to adopt a new set of skills. You will need not only new mindsets, but new heart-sets and skill-sets to match. Giving birth to a new way of being demands that you experiment with new partnerships, as well as new processes and ways of doing things. You'll have to get beyond, "Oh, I could never do that!" or "I've never done it this way!" Over time, you need to grow more comfortable in making mistakes as part of the messy nature of creativity and growth. Ultimately, it is less about thinking your way into a new way of being than it is acting your way into a new way of being.

For a community, it means becoming a learning community. Being a learning community requires letting go of the need to prove how much you already know. This involves breaking communal norms and parting from some of your time-honored traditions that chain you to the status quo and behaving in novel ways that are outside of your comfort zone. It involves trying things differently rather than just trying harder. It means making mistakes and learning from them, rather than casting blame and shaming one another when mistakes are made. It means acting your way into a new way of being, instead of succumbing to paralysis by analysis. Without experimenting and incubating new possibilities, risking new ventures, and partnering in new ways, there will be no transformation.

5. Transformative visioning: gather the wisdom, weave a dream

It is not the vision, per se, that transforms you, but the manner in which this visioning is done. Transformative Visioning is intended to gather the wisdom and weave a new dream. It involves listening to your deepest longings and greatest aspirations to create a new vision for the future. It requires letting go of what is no longer true, real or life-giving and listening to what is bringing forth new life. It is an organic, emergent and iterative process of discerning, listening to where the energy is, and continually visioning the future. It involves taking steps without having the full picture, seeing what emerges and taking the next best step in light of new understandings.

For communities this requires using more than just the conventional approaches to planning and visioning. When the problems are clear and the solutions are known, conventional approaches may be adequate. However, when engaged in deep change in search of new life, known maps and traditional ways of planning are inadequate. Communities need new approaches for planning and visioning, ones that will aid in the work of transformation, tap your deepest longings, promote meaning and create opportunities for new life to emerge. It is important to get beyond studying more articles and merely naming issues. You will need to work *through* issues and entertain wild and wonderful visions that take you to where new life has a chance.

REFLECTION 6: SHIFTS IN CONSCIOUSNESS

The real voyage of discovery consists not in seeking new landscapes,
but in having new eyes.
Marcel Proust

CREATING A NEW NARRATIVE

The Grand Canyon looks very different from the top than it does from the bottom. The perspective we might have while perched comfortably on the North Rim is very different than the one we would have if we were rafting down the rapids of the Colorado River. Our perspectives, thoughts and feelings change depending upon where we situate ourselves.

Deep change involves a shift in perspective. We need to resituate ourselves in order to unearth a new awareness and understanding of who we are, where we are, and our life's purpose. In order to break through from one way of thinking about our life to another, in order to write a new narrative for our lives, we need to shift the view we have of ourselves and our world.

One of the most challenging aspects of deep change are the constraints placed upon us by our own worldview. Our worldview tells us what is possible and what is not. It is our internal operating system that organizes what we see, hear, touch, taste and smell into our understanding. Our worldview shapes our mind-sets, informs our heart-sets and determines the skill-sets we employ. It is what determines whether we are pessimistic about the future or have hope for its possibilities. The inner work of transformation will invite you to adopt a new operating system, a new level of consciousness.

You might resonate with a desire to give birth to a new dream, yet have a hard time shaking free from your own worldview and attachments to the status quo. You might yearn for a new way forward, yet are blocked in imagining what the "new" might look like concretely. If you were to go through a transformation in your own life, what might emerge? You cannot know these things ahead of time, and you cannot engineer them, but you can create the conditions to allow newness to emerge.

One essential condition is an openness to adopting new perspectives for understanding the challenges we face. When seeing through a new lens, we discover that what we thought was creating our impasse or powerlessness, is not the whole reality. We have our hand on only one part of the elephant and miss the whole of it. Shifting perspectives is like twisting a kaleidoscope. It is the same stuff inside (i.e., rocks and mirrors), but with a slight twist, a whole new image appears. Similarly, a slight twist in the lens through which we look at our life, can bring forth a whole new perspective and understanding.

When we begin to see things differently, they don't have a hold on us as they once did. We are free to move again, whereas before we were stuck. Any lens that frees us might do. We can trick the mind if that is all we want to do. However, the transformation which we are addressing is not about mind games. The lenses that serve us well, that bring us to greater maturity and closer to God, are those that help us gaze into the soul. Nietzsche once said, "We look at the world thru different windows." What are the windows of your soul? What scripture passages or spiritual sages are stirring your soul today, shifting your perspectives and opening you up to new ventures?

MEDITATIONS

Thich Nhat Hanh

The past is alive in the Present Moment. The future is being shaped in the present moment; take good care of the present moment. Transform it. Live it…so that our earth, our children, will have a future.

Albert Einstein

We can't solve problems by using the same kind of thinking we used when we created them.

Teilhard de Chardin

For those who know how to see, everything is sacred.

Mark 2:22

No one pours new wine into old wineskins. Otherwise, the wine will burst the skins, and both the wine and the wineskins will be ruined. No, they pour new wine into new wineskins.

1 Corinthians 13:12

For now we see only a reflection as in a mirror; then we shall see face to face. Now I know in part; then I shall know fully, even as I am fully known.

Julian of Norwich. Showings

And in this he showed me something small, no bigger than a hazelnut, lying in the palm of my hand, and I perceived that it was as round as any ball. I looked at it and thought; What can it be? And I was given this general answer: It is everything which is made. I was amazed that it could last, for I thought that it was so little that it could suddenly fall into nothing. And I was answered in my understanding: It lasts and always will, because God loves it; and thus every-thing has being through the love of God. In this little thing I saw three properties. The first is that God made it, the second is that God loves it, and third is that

God preserves it...I am so attached to him that there can be no created thing between my God and me.

Journal Reflections and Exercises

Return to your first reflection regarding your own transformative experiences. Recall an old script about yourself and your life that you began to recognize, at some point, was constraining, disempowering or no longer fitting the truth of who you were. Whose voice was it that gave you this script (e.g., your mother, father, significant other)? Who told you, for example, that you were not "good enough," "smart enough," or "worthy enough?"

In contrast, whose voice spoke to you about a new script (e.g., your mother, father, significant other), or provided a new lens with which to understand who you truly were? What new perspectives began to emerge that helped you see a deeper truth about yourself and the life you were living? Recall who companioned you and what helped the emergence of a new script, your new life's story.

1. Describe the false narratives. When you had reached a cross-roads, what were the stories you had been telling yourself about your life that were no longer true? These were the stories, scrips that formed your self-image and directed your life in ways that were contrary to your emerging true self, to your new reality and new identity. They kept you from believing in yourself. They kept you boxed in and unfree. What were those stories?

2. Identify the truth-tellers. Who believed in you when you were at a point that you could no longer believe in yourself and what did they see in you that you could not see in yourself?

   a. For example, how did you come to know that you were, in fact, lovable, when you may have previously thought of yourself as unlovable or not good enough?

3. Test the truth. How were you sure that this new way of seeing yourself was actually true and not some type of false reassurance

given to you by someone trying to bolster your ego and help you feel better?

4. Look through the new lenses. What new lenses from nature, scripture, art, books, or people you knew did you find liberating, offering you new perspectives and stirring your soul toward new growth?

WISDOM FROM THE PAST, APPLIED TO THE PRESENT

Having reflected upon a past personal experience of transformation, gather the insights and learnings and apply it to the present. If your community is currently engaged in the work of transformation, answer the same reflection questions from the perspective of the community as a whole. If you are currently going through your own personal transformation, answer the same reflection questions as applied to you today.

Communal transformation

1. What are the stories your community continually tells itself, or others say about you, that are no longer true?

2. Who is now telling your community a true story about being valuable, good enough, worthy and lovable?

3. How do you know these voices are speaking the truth and not some kind of false reassurance?

4. What new lenses and perspectives are liberating your community and stirring its soul?

Personal transformation

1. What are the stories you tell yourself, or others say about you, that are no longer true?

2. Who is telling you a true story about being valuable, good enough, worthy and lovable?

3. How do you know these voices are true and not some kind of false reassurance?

4. What new lenses and perspectives are liberating you and stirring your soul?

REFLECTION 7: RECLAIMING YOUR INNER VOICE

There is nothing neutral about the soul. It is the seat and the source of life. Either we respond to what the soul presents in its fantasies and desires, or we suffer from this neglect of ourselves.
Thomas Moore. Care of the Soul

THE SEAT AND SOURCE OF EVERYTHING THAT LIVES

Thomas Moore suggests that, "Faith is a gift of spirit that allows the soul to remain attached to its own unfolding." When we are at a crossroads in life and are immersed in crisis, we have reached the point where our soul has lost its connection to its own unfolding. There is a disconnect between how we are living our life and how we are meant to live. There is a disconnect between the persona we project and our own true identity. Our life is out of alignment and detached from its soul. Theodore Roethke captures the torment of this disconnect: "What is madness but nobility of soul at odds with circumstance. The day is on fire and I know the purity of pure despair."

The inner work of transformation is the work of reclaiming, re-authenticating and re-aligning our soul with our life. Transformative experiences in life are near-death experiences of the soul. We awaken from the madness and despair just in the nick of time, having already paid a terrible price. The cost of reclaiming our soul, however, remains enormous. It is the pearl of great price. We reach a point at the crossroads where we realize that the price for reclaiming this pearl of new life is one we must pay; otherwise, we pay an unimaginable price of death without redemption.

At these "do or die" times, we are willing to risk losses we previously thought unbearable, even risking life itself, in order to reclaim our soul. We are willing to bear the pain of losing who we had once been or who we had once loved. We know we must let die what needs to die in order to bring to life our new self, in order to live more fully aligned with who God intends for us to become. We pay the price because the alternative is unthinkable.

To re-authenticate your soul means to reclaim your true self and make it manifest in your life. It means realigning your life in accord with your soul's deepest longings. It means growing into a more mature faith, "that you may fulfill God's will for you." (Colossians 4:12). Let your soul speak and show itself as it truly is and not as you wish it to be or what you wish others would see.

Re-authenticating your soul is more about the care of your soul than about some kind of cure. It is your ongoing attentiveness to your inner voice that has been neglected or overshadowed by egoic pursuits of temporal satisfactions. Listen for the deeper, eternal stories of your life's unfolding, not the temporal. The words of John O'Donohue say it well, "I would love to live like a river flows, carried by the surprise of its own unfolding."

MEDITATIONS

Parker Palmer. Let Your Life Speak

*Like a wild animal, the soul is tough, resilient, resourceful, savvy, and self-suf-
ficient: it knows how to survive in hard places. I learned about these qualities
during my bouts with depression. In that deadly darkness, the faculties I had
always depended on collapsed. My intellect was useless; my emotions were dead;
my will was impotent; my ego was shattered. But from time to time, deep in the
thickets of my inner wilderness, I could sense the presence of something that
knew how to stay alive even when the rest of me wanted to die. That something
was my tough and tenacious soul.*

Romans 8:19-22

*For the creation waits with eager longing for the revealing of the sons of God.
For the creation was subjected to futility, not willingly, but because of him who
subjected it, in hope that the creation itself will be set free from its bondage to
corruption and obtain the freedom of the glory of the children of God. For we
know that the whole creation has been groaning together in the pains of child-
birth until now.*

Ted Loder. Drive Me Deep to Face Myself

*Lord, grant me your peace, for I have made peace with what does not give me
peace and I am afraid.*
*Drive me deep, now, to face myself so I may see that what I truly need to
fear is…*
my capacity to deceive and willingness to be deceived,
my loving of things and using of people,
my struggle for power and shrinking of soul,
my addiction to comfort and sedation of conscience,
my readiness to criticize and reluctance to create,
my clamor for privilege and silence at injustice,
my seeking for security and forsaking the kingdom.
Lord, grant me your peace. Instill in me such fear of you as will begin to make

me wise,

and such quiet courage as will enable me to begin to make hope visible, forgiving delightful, loving contagious, faith liberating, peace-making joyful and myself open and present to the other people and your kingdom.

Nan C. Merrill. Psalms for Praying

For I seem ready to fall, my pain is always with me.
I confess my shortcomings, I am sorry for my transgression.
With mercy, You shed light into my darkness,
I can hide no longer behind the shield of ignorance.
Those who choose to live in the darkness are my adversaries,
because I choose now to walk in the light.

Richard Rohr. On the Threshold of Transformation: Daily Meditations for Men

Shadowy material resides inside each one of us, but the man who is willing to face his own capacity for darkness will discover his deepest inner goodness and the presence of the divine within him. Some men never discover the divine presence within because they can't bring themselves to face their demons. Don't try to engineer this process or manufacture any angels. It will be done to you; just do not hate or fear the falling.

Diarmuid O'Murchu. Adult Faith

Perhaps the single greatest challenge in this transformative process is the need to reclaim the vulnerable adult. This in fact is the inner self we have known over millions of years of our earlier evolution as a human species. Vulnerability is a graced gift. It keeps us close to the tenderness and fragility of all living organisms. It keeps us more open and receptive to the surprise of the new. And it alerts us to the dangerous allurement of heroic power games.

JOURNAL REFLECTIONS AND EXERCISES

By soul, I mean the quintessential essence of our being, our ultimate place in the universe, where God and I are joined. We cannot really identify one's soul from social roles or job titles. None of these get to the mysterious core of our identity. Any attempt to define our own soul would not suffice as a distillation of life experiences, the collective significance that is the soul. And by place in this universe, I mean the integral part we play in Creation, in God's unfolding dream – our true vocation.

1. Your soul. Although the ineffable soul confounds us all, how do you understand what is your own soul and the part you are to play in God's unfolding dream?

2. Your soulwork. Go back to your crossroads reflections regarding your own experiences of transformation:

   a. What was the soulwork you did at that time?

   b. What was your pearl of great price and what did it cost you?

   c. What did you choose to let die (e.g., relationships, attitudes, false personas, or pursuits) and what new life emerged as a result?

3. Your soul's stirrings. From the depth of your soul that stirred at night, or in the silent moments of your daytime musings, was there something you needed to hear?

   a. What was your soul saying to you during those times?

   b. What parts of your soul were detached or misaligned from your own life?

   c. How were you caring for your own soul and what was the soulwork you were being asked to do?

WISDOM FROM THE PAST, APPLIED TO THE PRESENT

Having reflected upon a past personal experience of transformation, gather the insights and learnings and apply it to the present. If your community is currently engaged in the work of transformation, answer the same reflection questions from the perspective of the community as a whole. If you are currently going through your own personal transformation, answer the same reflection questions as applied to you today.

Communal transformation

1. How do you understand what the soul of your community is and the part it is playing in God's unfolding dream?

2. What is the soulwork your community needs to do?

3. What do you hear stirring in the soul of your community?

Personal transformation

1. How do you understand what is your soul and the part it is playing today in God's unfolding dream?

2. What is the soulwork you now need to do?

3. What do you hear stirring in your own soul?

Reflection 8:
Reconciliation
and Conversion

I will give you a new heart and put a new spirit in you; I will remove from you
your heart of stone and give you a heart of flesh.
Ezekiel 36:26

THE WOMB OF OUR BECOMING

When we become separated from our true self, we are no longer whole. When parts of our true self have been lost, hidden or projected onto others, we live fragmented lives. We act one way at home, another way at work, and still another way with our friends. With some people we are truer to ourselves and with others we are imposters playing a role. We work in settings that are at odds with our basic values. We harbor secrets and manipulate information we share for our personal gain. We hide our beliefs from those with whom we disagree because we are afraid of being judged or causing conflict. We conceal our true identity and live inauthentic, unintegrated lives. Sooner or later, this house of cards collapses, and we fall into grace.

When we hit bottom, reach a point where we have nothing further of value to lose and decide that enough is enough, we are faced with the choice of whether or not to reconcile our brokenness. We are left to walk the long road in search of our hidden wholeness. Our task is to reckon with the brokenness we have experienced in ourselves or between our self and others. This road to healing and wholeness is the crucible of transformation. It is where we forge character and ripen our souls. It is the most painful and profitable work of transformation.

Reconciliation and conversion occur in more places than the chapel and with more people than spiritual directors or counselors. Private conversations with God are essential. Still, these are insufficient for completing the work of reconciliation. Perhaps you can repair your own heart in prayer, but you cannot heal a ruptured relationship by prayer alone. There are personal, interpersonal, and communal dimensions to this work and missing any one of these will render your work incomplete.

Most of us wish to avoid this work like the plague because it peels off the scab from wounds we'd rather not re-expose. We'd rather let these wounds scab over and forget about them. But this will not heal our soul. It will remain bruised and new reminders of similar incidents will only reinjure the soul and deepen these wounds. Yet, avoidance of our personal work is nothing compared to our avoidance of the *interpersonal* and *communal* work of reconciliation. This level of vulnerability brings greater risk and reward, but the risk of being hurt is a bridge too far for many, the reward forsaken. Predictably, new reminders of similar incidents reinjure the souls of all involved. The relationships and community itself are left wounded. We move on down the road, damage done, baggage in hand.

The inner work of conversion starts with a loving confrontation between God and our inner most self. Then we take the next step of reconciling and healing the relationships in our life that have been injured. This interpersonal reconciliation is a necessary step to restore our hidden wholeness in ourselves, our relationships and the community.

MEDITATIONS

Henri Nouwen. Darkness And The Dawn

The rabbi asked his students: "How can we determine the hour of dawn, when the night ends and the day begins?" One of the rabbi's students suggested: "When from a distance you can distinguish between a dog and a sheep?" "No," was the answer of the rabbi.

"It is when one can distinguish between a fig tree and a grapevine? Asked a second student. "No," the rabbi said. "Please tell us the answer then," said the students.

"It is then," said the wise teacher, "when you can look into the face of another human being and you have enough light in you to recognize your brother or your sister. Until then it is night. And darkness is still within us."

Ronald Rolheiser. Holy Longing

To say, "I don't have to deal with this!" goes against the teaching of Christ because this is precisely what he was referring to when he said: "Unless you eat my flesh you cannot have life within you." Jesus, at least in John's gospel is clear. We cannot bypass a flawed family on earth to try to relate to a nonflawed God in heaven. Concrete community is a nonnegotiable element with the spiritual quest because, precisely, we are Christians, not simply theists.

1 John 1:9-10

If we confess our sins, he is faithful and just and will forgive us our sins and purify us from all unrighteousness. If we claim we have not sinned, we make him out to be a liar and his word is not in us.

Matthew 5:23-26

So if you are offering your gift at the altar and there remember that your brother has something against you, leave your gift there before the altar and go. First be reconciled to your brother, and then come and offer your gift. Come to terms quickly with your accuser while you are going with him to court, lest your accuser hand you over to the judge, and the judge to the guard, and you be put in prison. Truly, I say to you, you will never get out until you have paid the last penny.

Joan Chittister. A Spirituality for the 21st Century

We can kneel and kneel and kneel but nothing changes because kneeling is not what we need to soften our souls just then. We can fast and kneel and tithe and nothing changes because we do not really want anything to change. Growth is not an accident. Growth is a process. We have to want to grow. We have to will to move away the stones that entomb us in ourselves. We have to work at uprooting the weeds that are smothering good growth in ourselves…Benedict trusts us to make a choice to discipline ourselves somehow, someway, so that we do not sink into the mire of self-satisfaction so thick that there is no rescue for our sated souls.

JOURNAL REFLECTIONS AND EXERCISES

Intra-personal reconciliation and conversion

The inner work of transformation invites us to make whole again what was once whole, but has since become fragmented. We are asked to reckon with our growing hypocrisy and the disconnect between our soul and our life. We are urged to face our fears, guilt and shame. At one level, we do this hard, inner work of reckoning because the pain of not doing it is unbearable. We are comforted in this work because we know deep down of God's unconditional love, the love we wish to offer others, and the hidden wholeness that lies beneath these unreconciled parts of our soul.

1. Personal healing. Return to your reflections on your crossroads identified in Part III. What was the personal healing you had to do, and how did you do it? In what ways were you made more whole by the inner work you did?

Inter-personal reconciliation and conversion

It is one thing to acknowledge our personal shortcomings in the privacy of our own prayers, our own journaling, or in the company of a spiritual guide or therapist. It is quite another matter to face those we have wounded or by whom we have been wounded. Reconciliation means engaging those with whom we have exchanged wounds by a lack of honesty or compassion, mean-spirited judgments, irresponsible behavior or misunderstandings. Reconciliation includes facing the persons we love with the recognition that our love has sometimes failed. Conversion happens when we face those who have perpetrated violence against us and we find forgiveness in our hearts. The only ones who can reconcile the wounds of a faith community are the members of the community themselves.

1. Interpersonal healing. What have been some of the interpersonal work of mending relationships in community in the past? How have you attended to the interpersonal work of reconciliation and transformation (or have you)?

WISDOM FROM THE PAST, APPLIED TO THE PRESENT

Having reflected upon a past personal experience of transformation, gather the insights and learnings and apply it to the present. If your community is currently engaged in the work of transformation, answer the same reflection questions from the perspective of the community as a whole. If you are currently going through your own personal transformation, answer the same reflection questions as applied to you today.

Communal transformation

1. What are the wounds in community that require healing in order to restore the community's hidden wholeness?

2. How are you attending to this interpersonal work of reconciliation and healing?

Personal transformation

1. What wounds are you carrying that require healing in order to restore your own hidden wholeness?

2. How are you attending to this personal work of reconciliation and healing?

Reflection 9:
Experimentation
and Learning

For our lives to be meaningful, they must succeed in continuing the creative work of evolution.
Teilhard de Chardin

Acting our way into a new way being

How did you learn how to play an instrument, a new sport, speak a new language, dance, sing, or learn any acquired skill in life? These are not skills you acquired from a book, but from experience. Reading may have given you some good ideas, but it was in your practicing, fumbling, and refining that you gained proficiency. How did you learn to love, to live in community, to team with others, to be with God or any of these ways of relating? These are not skills you learned in a book. These, too, are learned from experience.

I'm not knocking education. I went as far as I could in school and I am a voracious reader with a desk buried in books. But as much as I read, study and Google my way to new information, none of those hours spent have given me a shred of wisdom or matured me in any way. Books can give you knowledge, but wisdom comes from experience and experience is what transforms you. Books can prepare you, help you understand things, give you new ideas, but transformation is the soul's lived experience of maturation. The inner work of transformation invites you to *act your way into a new way of being*, not think your way into a new way of acting.

Sometimes when we have a new insight, we attempt to act upon it with new behaviors. At other times, we "act out" in new ways without consciously understanding why. We intuit our way forward, acting out of our emergent impulses without much discipline, understanding or finesse. It isn't always pretty, successful or socially accepted. This is why adolescents get in a lot of trouble for their acting out. Yet, look at how much growth occurs during adolescence! We act out growth urges before we even understand what is impelling us. Learning by doing is the way we evolve. Transformation is evolution in action.

Carl Jung once said, "The greatest and most important problems of life are fundamentally unsolvable. They can never be solved, but only outgrown." Maturation is not a problem to be solved. Mystery is not a problem to be solved. These are not the matters of our mind, but the substance of our soul. Our soul cannot ripen without taking new risks in our behavior.

The inner work of transformation requires risking outward experimentation with new behaviors. This is where life is lived: in mission, in community and with our family and friends. The inner work of our soul's search for growth must include changing patterns of interaction with others, such as, giving voice when we have typically gone silent, or being silent when we've typically spoken up. Breaking norms, trying new behaviors, and creating new patterns are our life's experiments in transformation. Thich Nhat Hanh says it this way: "Our own life is the instrument with which we experiment with truth." The inner work of transformation invites us to experiment with the truth by acting in new ways.

MEDITATIONS

Neale Donald Walsh. Conversations with God

Yearning for a new way will not produce it. Only ending the old way can do that. You cannot hold onto the old, all the while declaring that you want something new. The old will defy the new; the old will deny the new; the old will decry the new. There is only one way to bring in the new. You must make room for it.

Richard Rohr. Falling Upward

Mature religion involves changing ourselves and letting ourselves be changed by the mysterious encounter with grace, mercy, and forgiveness. This is the truth that will set us free.

Ephesians 4:13-15

...Until we all attain to the unity of the faith, and of the knowledge of the Son of God, to a mature man, to the measure of the stature which belongs to the fullness of Christ. As a result, we are no longer to be children, tossed here and there by waves and carried about by every wind of doctrine, by the trickery of men, by craftiness in deceitful scheming; but speaking the truth in love, we are to grow up in all aspects into Him who is the head, even Christ.

Margaret Wheatley

Strict obedience and compliance destroys creativity.

Joan Chittister. Between the Dark and the Daylight

Failure gives us the chance to experiment with life, to play with it a bit, to move in different directions until we find, as we learned from Cinderella as children, the shoe that fits. Because what doesn't fit will irritate us all our life. We will live in the unnecessary pain that comes from forcing ourselves into something that not only embarrasses us but cramps our hearts and damps our spirits.

JOURNAL REFLECTIONS AND EXERCISES

Return to your first reflection regarding your own transformative experiences in life.

1. Acting out: What "acting out" took place during your own time of transformation? What did you do before you were even prepared or understood what was even happening? What steps were taken, however clumsy and painful, that were steps you took in the right direction?

2. New skills and behaviors: Sometimes, we know how we wish to grow, but we have not yet acquired the behaviors that match our newly discovered insights. We might look to others, or associate with new friends or mentors who have these skills and exhibit these behaviors. What new behaviors did you seek to acquire, or new skills did you have to learn, in order to grow and emerge more fully as your true self, and from whom did you learn these?

3. Unlearning: Transformation is often more about unlearning than learning. What was the most important thing you had to unlearn in order to grow and transform as you did?

4. The experience of fumbling: What was it like for you to fumble and fail in the acquisition of new skills and in your experimentation with new behaviors? How did you handle this? How did you self-correct and recover?

WISDOM FROM THE PAST, APPLIED TO THE PRESENT

Having reflected upon a past personal experience of transformation, gather the insights and learnings and apply it to the present. If your community is currently engaged in the work of transformation, answer the same reflection questions from the perspective of the community as a whole. If you are currently going through your own personal transformation, answer the same reflection questions as applied to you today.

Communal transformation

1. In what ways might your community be acting out an urge toward new life?

2. What new skills or behaviors need to be acquired and how might your community acquire these?

3. What are things your community must unlearn in order to make room for the new?

4. What has been your community's experience of fumbling and how are you handling it?

Personal transformation

1. In what ways might you be acting out an urge toward new life?

2. What new skills or behaviors do you need to acquire and how might you acquire these?

3. What things must you unlearn in order to make room for the new?

4. What has been your experience of fumbling and how are you handling it?

REFLECTION 10: TRANSFORMATIVE VISIONING

Your walking, your footprints are the road, and nothing else; there is no road, walker, you make the road by walking. By walking you make the road, and when you look backward, you see the path that you never will step on again. Walker, there is no road, only wind-trails in the sea.
Antonio Machado. Proverbs and Tiny Songs

GATHER THE WISDOM, WEAVE A DREAM

Transformative Visioning is the linchpin that connects the other four dynamic elements through a process of creating a future that is distinct from your past. It is the manner in which you give life to your deepest longings and greatest aspirations. It is the overarching movement through which the other four dynamic elements in the Journey of Transformation are woven together and made manifest. Your inner work here is to give expression to your truest selves by the future you seek to create and by the manner in which you shape it.

When we move through a transformative experience in life, we discover, or rediscover in new ways, that which is our true purpose in life. We understand our calling in a new way and we claim a new path. There is no grand plan mapped out ahead of time. Rather, we know deep down that we are taking a step toward a new direction and that somehow our life will never be the same. When you joined Religious Life, or made any major commitment, did you map it out with a strategic plan? Did you have goals and objectives laid out across a timeline? Probably not.

These life-changing commitments are always a leap of faith. New paths, those pursued by restless souls, are always made by walking. Our manner of visioning is *emergent* in that each step taken toward our soul's desires reveals new insights, greater clarity and a better understanding of how to move next. Our way of visioning is *organic* in that it is truly a maturational process of growth, not a grand plan of our own architectural design. Of equal, if not greater, importance than what we actually shape is the manner in which we go about it. The process of creating a vision is itself transformative: trusting in the grace of God to lead us; creating new partnerships and companions along the way; discovering the abundant gifts we didn't know we had; and stretching our souls in new ways.

Henry David Thoreau once said, "Our truest life is when we are in our dreams awake." When our soul connects to our deepest longings, when we are awake and consciously allow our longings to inform how we move into the future, then we are allowing ourselves to be transformed as we walk. If we stifle our longings and keep hope from rising, we risk the loss of new life. Michelangelo put it this way: "The greatest danger for most of us is not that our aim is too high and we miss it, but that it is too low and we reach it." Aim high. Bring to life to your greatest aspirations!

MEDITATIONS

Rainer Maria Rilke

You must give birth to your images. They are the future waiting to be born. Fear not the strangeness you feel. The future must enter you long before it happens. Just wait for the birth for the hour of new clarity.

Revelation 21:1-3, 5a

Then I saw new heavens and a new earth. The former heavens and the former earth had passed away, and the sea was no longer. I also saw a new Jerusalem, the holy city, coming down out of heaven from God, beautiful as a bride prepared to meet her husband. I heard a loud voice from the throne cry out: "This is God's dwelling among men. He shall dwell with them, and they shall be his people and he shall be their God who is always with them." The One who sat on the throne said to me: "See, I make all things new!"

JOURNAL REFLECTIONS AND EXERCISES

Once again, return to your earlier reflections recalling transformative experiences in your life and explore the following questions.

1. Deepest longings: What were your deepest longings that lured you toward some future aspiration or vision?

2. Mana: When you claimed a new path of life, what told you that you were moving in the right direction? What nourished you and kept you moving forward when its destination could not be known?

3. Course-corrections: What course-corrections did you need to make along the way and how did your vision of a future morph and change over time? Did you ever imagine it would turn out as it did?

4. The way: What was it about the way in which you shaped your future that stretched your soul and helped you become the person you are today?

WISDOM FROM THE PAST, APPLIED TO THE PRESENT

Having reflected upon a past personal experience of transformation, gather the insights and learnings and apply it to the present. If your community is currently engaged in the work of transformation, answer the same reflection questions from the perspective of the community as a whole. If you are currently going through your own personal transformation, answer the same reflection questions as applied to you today.

Communal transformation

1. What are your deepest longings and greatest aspirations for the future of your community?

2. What are the signs telling you that your community is moving in the right direction?

3. What course-correction might your community need to make right now?

4. What will help stretch your community's soul to become new again?

Personal transformation

1. What are your deepest longings and greatest aspirations for your own future?

2. What are the signs telling you that you are moving in the right direction?

3. What course-correction might you need to make in your own journey right now?

4. What will help stretch your own soul to become new again?

PART V: LIFE REVIEW

*Some time when the river is ice ask me mistakes I have made. Ask me
whether what I have done is my life. Others have come in their slow way into
my thought, and some have tried to help or to hurt: ask me what difference
their strongest love or hate has made. I will listen to what you say. You and I
can turn and look at the silent river and wait. We know the current is there,
hidden; and there are comings and goings from miles away that hold the stillness exactly before us. What the river says, that is what I say.*
William Stafford. Ask me

UNFINISHED BUSINESS OF OUR LIVES

When St. John of the Cross died, December 14, 1591, he repeated the words
of the psalmist, "Into your hands, O Lord I commend my spirit." He had been
through his own dark night and was ready to receive God in a new way. Much
of his readiness came from the confinement of his dark and cramped prison
cell. It was there, out of his own mystical experience, he wrote the first thir-
ty-one stanzas of *The Spiritual Canticle*. In it, he described the urgent longings of a lover searching for her beloved: "Where have you hidden, Beloved,

and left me moaning? You fled like the stag, after wounding me; I went out calling, and you were gone."

Listen to the ache and imagine the panic he was feeling as he wrote those words! Have you ever, in your own life, felt such torment and panic? This is the fuel that stirs the soul and impels us to examine our own misgivings. The losses, regrets, and unhealed wounds we carry within us are painful reminders of just how unfinished our soulwork is. These unredeemed aspects of our life invite us to the inner work of transformation. It is the desperate search to be reunited, our God and true self conjoined, that impels us to spiral deeper into the recesses of our soul. Only this ache can override our reluctance to address our unhealed wounds that keep us separated from God.

The inner work of transformation has a great deal to do with our addressing the unhealed parts of our soul that separate us from God and from those we love. Here, we are invited to work with the "unfinished business" we have accumulated and to clean out the clutter that sullies our soul, dulls our passion and dims any vision we might, otherwise, have for the future. Part V of this guide invites you to focus on the unhealed wounds, unshaken regrets and grieving that may reside deep within your heart. It is an invitation to review your life in these areas and then to replenish the unclaimed abundance and gratitude in your life.

These areas are not everyone's unfinished business. But it may give you a start in your own life review. Once you get started on these areas– grief, forgiveness, regrets, abundance, and gratitude– you might wish to address other aspects of unfinished business.

REFLECTION 11: GRIEF

And sooner or later, with more or less pain, we all must come to know that loss is indeed a lifelong human condition.
Judith Viorst. Necessary Losses

A LABOR OF LETTING GO

The stages of human growth and development have been described by Confucius, Shakespeare, Erikson and countless others. Periods of stability wherein we solidify our identity, worldview and life circumstances are invariably punctuated by periods of transition wherein our prior arrangements are brought into question. Letting go of what were our measures of success, markers of identity, and attachments that mattered, is part of the inner work required for transformation and growth to occur.

Grieving is the labor of letting go in order to make room for the "new." Grieving is also a source of wisdom and a catalyst for maturation. Every faith tradition knows that, in the renunciation of that which shaped us before, the spiritual quest for "the more" begins. Grieving is the inner work of transformation that opens the door to the more.

No one could deny that the longer we live, and the more years we accumulate, the more losses we face along the way. We will mourn the loss of those we loved along the way, but we must also mourn the loss of identity as we grow – earlier definitions of self, roles, titles, aspirations and abilities, deep beliefs and attachments of all kinds, and eventually our physical and mental capacities. We will lose our health, our home and our havens. We lose our jobs and, along with these, our status and our purposefulness. The first half of life seems marked by accumulating, accomplishing, and producing while the latter half by letting go, dismantling and surrendering. The better able we are to grieve, the more of life we can continue take in, the better we can love and the larger our soul becomes.

Hospice workers tell us that those who are more at peace during the dying process are those that have done their inner work of grieving life's losses along the way. Shakespeare would agree that the failure to mourn is hazardous to your health, "Give sorrow words: the grief that does not speak whispers the oe'r fraught heart, and bids it break." But you don't have to be a poet or hospice worker to know that grieving is disordered when it is delayed or denied in order to avoid the pain.

When our past realities start to collapse, and we are about to lose a cherished hobby, a fulfilling ministry, or someone we loved, we, sometimes, assail this loss by refusing to adapt. We become change-resisters rather than agents of change, digging in our heels, and defying the reality by distracting ourselves with busyness. When we don't mourn, the necessary losses in life, we somaticize and become ill, cling and close in on ourselves, or perhaps anesthetize our pain with addictions. We become affectively blunted and emotionally stunted.

However, if we truly mourn, if we grieve our life's losses when we encounter them, then, on the other side of it, there is liberation. Grieving is the inner work of transforming the pain of loss into the possibility of new life. It is a lifeforce energy that spawns wisdom, empathy and compassion, a catalyst for our soul's evolution.

MEDITATIONS

E. M. Forster

We must be willing to let go of the life we have planned, so as to have the life that is waiting for us.

Matthew 5:4

Blessed are those who mourn, for they will be comforted.

Psalm 46:1-2

God is our refuge and strength, an ever-present help in trouble. Therefore we will not fear, though the earth give way and the mountains fall into the heart of the sea.

Kelly Ann Hall. Enough of You

Bless us O, God, with enough of You to bring us out of hiding undressed of untruths, thin as leaves, and bare to our souls to be known. Even as nerves are unwrapped and anxieties un-bandaged, even with our instinctual desire to cloak, to tailor a way out of exposure and cheat our way out of certain death, we come out to You not because it's easy...because hiding is futile. Nothing goes unnoticed, nothing unseen—there is not one thing that exists outside of Your vision. So, we give You our willingness to be vulnerable, to become transparent and teachable, to be redesigned and redressed. To our greatest ability, God, we bring ourselves to You, hoping you will take us as we are.

JOURNAL REFLECTIONS AND EXERCISES

While Kübler Ross described five universal phases of grief (denial, anger, bargaining, depression and acceptance), each person's inner work of grieving is unique. These stages easily overlap and intermingle with one another. How you mourn your losses, therefore, needs to be a path of your own making. Below are some suggestions upon which you can build and shape your own path to grieving.

Name and claim the losses

Jot down two or three losses that you have experienced in the past or are now facing. Jot down the ones that you have yet to fully grieve, the ones that are keeping you from being fully alive, are blunting your passion or numbing your soul. Name and claim these losses for yourself and choose one that you wish to address now.

Write a letter

If this was a person you lost, or are at risk of now losing, perhaps you can write a letter to them. Describe what they meant to you, the struggles in your relationship, how they enriched your life and how you have grown (or hope to grow) as a result. Offer or ask for forgiveness. Make promises of how you intend to live going forward. Share what your life would have been like in the future had they been a part of it and what it will be like without them. Share anything that is in your heart. Scream your anger, lament your sadness, and express your guilt or whatever emotions arise.

You could go a step further by sharing this letter directly with them if they are available and receptive to this. If they are now gone, you might wish to share this letter with someone you believe could witness and support you in your grieving. Alternatively, you could write a letter addressed to someone else whom you know cares deeply about you, someone who could empathize with your loss and understand your pain (Jesus, a parent, or close friend). Share this letter with them, or another witness, and ask for their support.

Transform the disempowering messages into empowering ones

A profound loss will never be grieved to the point of erasing all of its pain. Reminders will always reawaken some of the pain. The pain that remains, however, can either be a source of empowerment or disempowerment. It can be part of your emotional aliveness and help you empathize with others' pain or it can be a source of hopelessness, despair and a barrier to intimacy. Journal about how your loss has been both empowering and disempowering to your spirit. Rewrite the disempowering messages into more empowering ones.

Ritualize letting go

Sometimes, we are almost ready to let go, but need to do something beyond words to help us turn the corner. Rituals can do what words cannot in helping us cross a threshold. Create your own ritual for that purpose. For example, find an object that symbolically represents the person, possession, attitude or belief you wish to release more fully and what you wish to take with you as you move forward. Perhaps you wish to bury, burn or give away the symbolic object you need to let go while blessing and finding a special place for the object you will carry forth. Hold these objects in a special place in the days preceding the ritual in order to heighten your soul's awareness. Use prayer and symbols to mark your transition and key people as witnesses to support you in your passage.

REFLECTION 12: FORGIVENESS

There is no future without forgiveness.
Desmond Tutu

A LABOR OF LOVE

Conventional wisdom tells us, "Time heals all wounds." But experience tells us that wounds can just as easily fester and hearts can harden with the passage of time. Time itself is not the transformative agent, forgiveness is. Time simply provides the opportunity for healing, but we make choices whether or not to fester or forgive. While the rush of time quickens with age, as long as we are alive there is still time for forgiveness. It is a matter of choice.

Debunking myths of forgiveness

1. Forgiveness does not excuse or absolve the offender from the consequences of their actions; rather it places it squarely in their lap.

2. Forgiveness does not require that we resume the relationship, though it may open the door for that possibility.

3. Forgiveness is not an event; it is a process.

4. Forgiveness does not change the past or mean that we forget the past; rather it can keep us from being stuck in the past and helps us open up to the future.

5. Forgiveness does not mean relinquishing our right to feel hurt or angry; rather, it invites the expression and release of painful feelings that helps us to let go of them.

Forgiveness is a labor of love

Forgiveness is a labor of love that, over time, releases us from the pain of unhealed wounds: bitterness, rancor, resentment, hurt, sadness, guilt or shame. It is a labor of love that involves taking back our power and making choices to end our victimhood. It empowers us to forgive the offender and heal ourselves. It is what releases us from being stuck in the past and stewing in a toxic mix of emotions. Forgiveness is another doorway to growth and returns to us the control we have over our own happiness.

Forgiveness takes courage, discipline and persistence over time. It is an uphill choice, when the temptations of avoidance, denial and blame are so much easier. It is a choice to open up painful emotions, rather than shove them below the floorboards of our consciousness. Forgiveness is a labor of self-love that nourishes our personal growth and soul's ripening.

Genuine forgiveness is a labor of love for reconciling relationships. It is a choice to raise difficult conversations and risk unknown outcomes, knowing that silence would be so much easier but ultimately more wounding. It is a choice to do more than simply saying, "I'm sorry." The labor of forgiveness is a conversation that seeks empathic understanding. It is a dialogue that makes room for the pouring out and receiving of anguish. It is the sustained presence between two people intent on healing that melts hearts and turns bitterness, anger and shame into compassion.

Apologies, unaccompanied by these kinds of laborious and courageous conversations, amount to nothing more than empty words. Premature apologies abort genuine forgiveness that can only be arrived at through dialogue. Too often, saying, "I'm sorry" is simply a way of getting off the hot seat and putting an end to an otherwise uncomfortable conversation. "I'm sorry," if said too quickly, becomes a conversation stopper, rather than an olive branch extended once the layers of mutual empathy and compassion have been fully exchanged.

MEDITATIONS

Nelson Mandela

As I walked out of the door toward the gate that would lead to my freedom, I knew if I didn't leave my bitterness and hatred behind, I'd still be in prison.

Luke 6:37

Judge not, and you will not be judged; condemn not, and you will not be condemned; forgive, and you will be forgiven.

Proverbs 25:21

If your enemy is hungry, give him bread to eat, and if he is thirsty, give him water to drink.

Desmond Tutu and Mpho Tutu. Book of Forgiving

You have stood at this junction before; You will stand at this junction again
And if you pause you can ask yourself which way to turn
You can turn away from your own sadness and run the race named revenge
You will run that tired track again and again
Or you can admit your own pain and walk the path that ends
In this direction lies freedom, my friend; I can show you where hope and wholeness make their homes
But you can't push past your anguish on your way there
To find the path of peace You will have to meet your pain, and speak its name.

Richard Rohr. Just This

Grace is the secret, undeserved key whereby God, the Divine Locksmith, sets you free from your self-made prisons and merit-badge mentality. It shows itself as radical forgiveness—of reality in general-and then forgiveness of each individual thing-for not being perfect. This will change both your politics and your psychology. Without grace and forgiveness, everything human devolves into smallness, hurt, victimhood, and blame. When you stop all weighing and measuring, you are finally in the infinite ocean of God's grace. God is not very good at math— and does not even know how to count.

JOURNAL REFLECTIONS AND EXERCISES

Forgiving someone who has wounded you

Prepare your heart and not your case. Forgiving someone who has wounded you involves doing your own inner work to prepare your heart for forgiveness, not preparing your arguments to defend your case against them. Prepare your heart means looking at your own contributions to the difficulty and imagining what it is like if you were standing in the other person's shoes. Prepare your heart by readying yourself to face their wounds, and to express your regrets. It means preparing yourself to speak your hard truths and listening to theirs. Preparing your heart means garnering the discipline to sit in the hot seat long enough to give healing a chance.

Recall what happened and reclaim how you felt about it. Reflect upon, journal, or share with a confidant, what happened and relive the emotional impact of the events and words spoken in the wounding experience. Let the emotions spill out without censoring. Then invite the conversation with the person who wounded you. If you and the other person wish, ask for someone who is neutral and skilled to facilitate the conversation.

Forgiving someone who can't forgive you

What is perhaps harder than a face-to-face conversation is forgiving another who can't forgive you. Perhaps you wish to reconcile, but the other person refuses to talk with you or has died or moved away. If a conversation is impossible, or the other person is unwilling to reconcile, it leaves the burden to you. Someone's refusal to talk with you, whether intended as punishment or not, can reinforce your shame, bitterness or fears. However, it ought not leave you stuck. You can still come to forgiveness, make amends and find peace in your own heart.

Write in your journal letting your thoughts and emotions spill out onto the page. Purge any thoughts and feelings that come to mind without censoring. Hold nothing back. Then put it away and let it rest a few days. Now write a more disciplined letter to the other person expressing your thoughts and emotions regarding the wounds that have occurred. This time, be careful to refrain from judgment, blame, or assuming you know what they feel or their motivations. Be honest, balancing your experience with what you imagine might have been theirs. The goal here is to do an honest and fair accounting, assuming responsibility for your part in it, owning your feelings about what happened, and offering forgiveness for whatever they may have said or done that caused you pain.

You may or may not wish to send this letter if they are refusing to talk with you. Unless you think there is a good chance that it might entice them to want to talk with you, it is better to err on the side of caution. Letters alone will not bring healing, but it might bring them to the conversation. Talk with a confidant and discern the pros and cons about this option. Would it cause more harm than good for them or for you? If the other person is deceased, you might wish to share your letter with a confidant or trusted friend.

Forgiving yourself for having wounded another

Self-forgiveness for having harmed another is often more difficult than forgiving another for having injured you. Write a letter to yourself describing what happened, taking responsibility for your part in it, forgiving yourself, committing to make amends, to learn and to grow from the experience. Alternatively, write a letter to yourself using the voice and perspective of the other person forgiving you. Step inside their shoes and imagine what they might say if they were to reconcile with you. Alternatively, write a letter to yourself as if it were written by someone who loves you (Jesus, a spiritual mentor, a parent, a caring friend). Self-forgiveness requires the same kind of compassion we naturally give to people we love. What would someone who genuinely loves you say to you about the pain you are experiencing?

Make amends, ritualize and let it go

Making amends can help release the pain, even if it cannot be done directly with the person involved in the conflict. Pay it forward to others who may be in similar circumstances. Alternatively, create a ritual involving the letter you wrote. Set the ritual in the context of prayer, include a supportive witness, and share your letter. Bury or burn the letter as a commitment to your letting go.

Reflection 13: Regrets

Soothing our regrets: Woulda, coulda, shoulda

The inner work of transformation challenges us to transform regrets into life lessons, rather than disempowering messages that remind us of our failings. Ruminating about past regrets can sound like woulda, coulda, shoulda: "I wish I *woulda* had the courage to live my life true to myself, not the life other people expected of me;" or "I wish I *coulda* stayed in touch with friends and family." or "I *shoulda* had the courage to express my feelings, without the fear of being rejected or unpopular." Regrets haunt us and follow us down the street like tin cans tied to our backs. Regrets nag at us and drag us down.

Regrets focus our attention on the past, deplete our energy to live in the present moment, and diminish our hope for the future: "I wish I would have forgiven someone when I had the chance. I wish I had told the people I loved the most how important they were to me. I wish I would have had more confidence and tried more things in life, instead of being so afraid of looking like a fool. I wish I would have done more to make an impact on this world." Enough!

By all means, it helps to look back at our lives and take full ownership for who we have been, but not for the purpose of adding up a long list of regrets. When we look back at what we could have done, should have done, or what we would have done differently had we known better, we can gather our life's lessons. The answers and insights from these life lessons can tell us who we really are and instruct us as to who we can become in the future. Instead of looking back with regret upon the choices you made that you wish you hadn't, let these life lessons tell you who you are growing to become, who God is calling you to become.

The benefit of a life review is the opportunity to shape a different, more empowering narrative for the future based upon what you now know of the life you have lived. The inner work of transformation invites you to turn regrets into life lessons, ones that also provide clues about your future aspirations. Let your regrets become newfound commitments for how you want to live your life going forward in the years you have remaining.

I'm not suggesting that you can actually live your life with no regrets. Regrets are part of the human condition. However, regrets can become toxins that eat away at our soul or sources of wisdom that ripen our soul. Regrets can reinforce our inadequacies and flawed nature or they can be teachers that point the way to a new way of being. The choice is yours.

MEDITATIONS

Joan Chittister. Gift Of Years

The burden of regret is that, unless we come to understand the value of the choices we made in the past, we may fail to see the gifts they have brought us. The blessing of regret is clear – it bring us, if we are willing to face it head on, to the point of being present to this new time of life in a an entirely new way. It urges us on to continue becoming.

Victoria Holt

Never regret. If it's good, it's wonderful. If it's bad, it's experience.

Job 3:3, 11

Let the day perish on which I was born, and the night that said, 'A man is conceived.' Why did I not die at birth, come out from the womb and expire?

Brian Rathbone

Wisdom is the reward for surviving our own stupidity.

Matthew 26:75

And Peter remembered the word which Jesus had said, 'Before a rooster crows, you will deny Me three times.' And he went out and wept bitterly.

Fabiana Fondevila. Grateful for the Lessons of Regret

How do we make room for our less graceful hours, the moments we wish we could rewrite, the subtle cop-outs, the inconsistencies? Can we find it in ourselves to appreciate our flailing efforts, to forgive our less than perfect courage, to recognize the aching heart that stood in our way? We aspire to be good people and we do not always make the mark. Yet there is in our strivings a strange sort of beauty. We struggle. We fail. We look back on our deeds. We rethink. We regret. We learn. And if we're lucky, this sends the wheel spinning forward in a slightly shifted direction. We, the imperfect creatures, are also those who can grow and change and sometimes make amends. It is an integral part of who we are. And the truth is, if we don't make peace with our vulnerability and our less endearing qualities, we run the risk of leading a shadow life, which amounts to a shallow life, one not fully inhabited. In doing so, we dismiss the very ground from which we can eventually climb up to higher heights, one sure-footed step at a time.

JOURNAL REFLECTIONS AND EXERCISES

The inner work of transforming regrets into life lessons starts with making the list and checking it twice. Create your laundry list of regrets that nag at you. Write down as many as you can, large or small, without censoring or analyzing these.

Now look across your list and cross off the ones that have the least hold on you until you have only three remaining. Now examine the list of regrets one more time and cross off two more, leaving the one that holds the most power over you. Your work is with the one regret remaining on your list. When you have worked through this one regret, you can always return to your list and rework another.

Review and recommit

1. Lessons Learned. What does this regret say about what kept you from making a better choice at the time? Are these same inhibitions or barriers still a part of you? Name these in writing. What might you do about these? Make a personal commitment over the coming year to apply these lessons by making new choices: "*This year I will…*"

2. Growth opportunities. What does this regret say about who you would have liked to have been and, therefore, who you'd rather be going forward? What choices can you make now in your life that are more aligned with how you want to be or are called to be? Make a personal commitment over the coming year to apply these lessons toward making new choices: "*This year I will…*"

3. Shadow work. Explore those parts of yourself you've tucked away and need to reclaim. What is the shadow side of your soul that you wish to redeem and strengthen in order to become more loving and more fully your true self? What might you need to do in order to work with these shadow parts of yourself? Who could help you with this inner work? Make a commitment to this work over the coming year: "*This year I will…*"

REFLECTION 14: ABUNDANCE

They sat down in groups of hundreds and of fifties. And He took the five loaves and the two fish, and looking up toward heaven, He blessed the food and broke the loaves and He kept giving them to the disciples to set before them; and He divided up the two fish among them all. They all ate and were satisfied.

Mark 6:41

FROM SCARCITY TO ABUNDANCE

More often than I care to admit, I feel as though who I am is not enough. "I'm not good enough," is an all too frequent refrain in my life. Sometimes, I find myself buying and accumulating things out of some vague notion that what I have is "not enough." From where does this sense of inadequacy, and perceived self-deprivation, originate? I have, by most standards, a good family, good health and a meaningful career. I was fortunate enough to be born in a great country and I expect to live longer than most men from other countries. Yet, too often, I live from a posture of scarcity, rather than abundance.

The inner work of transformation means shifting your mindset from scarcity to abundance. This inner work requires that you transpose those internalized worldly messages that signify you're "not good enough," to messages that reflect your true self, "made in the image of God" (Genesis 1:27). It means reframing scarcity into abundance by focusing more on what you do have rather than on what you are lacking, and calling it enough. It is more than enough. It is all you need. It is gift and it is blessing.

"And God is able to provide you with every blessing in abundance, so that by always having enough of everything, you may share abundantly in every good work" (2 Corinthians 9:8). God's economy is a gift economy based upon grace and love that is unmerited, free and enduring. It is not an economy of commodities based upon scarcity and competition. The inner work of transformation invites you to consider the choice regarding which "economy" you will engage in your life.

You are made in the image of God and you have an abundance. Do you believe this? Accept the hand you've been dealt. Claim it as yours. Celebrate what you have, the goodness in life, and claim it as yours. Today is gift. Your life, this day, is gift for your enjoyment. Thinking of it this way brings the only response it can –gratitude for the abundance. Spend this day as if it were you last day. Open your heart to life's blessings and let these blessings flow through you to the world. Let everyone you meet today be blessed by your presence and let your gratitude spill into the world.

MEDITATIONS

Derrick Carpenter. Crossroads

I came upon a crossroads where I sought only shelter for a brief time. But as I lay down my sack and kicked off my shoes, I noticed that this crossroads was like no other I had found. The air in this place held an inviting warmth and a vibrancy permeated all things. As I introduced myself to the travelers here, I felt no hesitation or discouragement but sincerity and optimism in their place. In their eyes I saw something I could not name but that felt very much like home. In this place, together, we shared and encouraged and rejoiced in the abundance of life.....

Luke 9:16

Then He took the five loaves and the two fish, and looking up to heaven, He blessed them, and broke them, and kept giving them to the disciples to set before the people.

Psalm 36-7-9

How precious is your steadfast love, O God! All people may take refuge in the shadow of your wings. They feast on the abundance of your house, and you give them drink from the river of your delights. For with you is the fountain of life; in your light we see light.

Rumi

Why are you so enchanted by this world, when a mine of gold lies within you?

2 Corinthians 9:8

God is able to make every grace abundant for you, so that in all things, always having all you need, you may have an abundance for every good work.

Walter Burghardt

Contemplation is a long, loving look at the real.

Brother David Steindl-Rast

See video: "A Grateful Day" (https://www.youtube.com/watch?v=zSt7k_q_qRU)

JOURNAL REFLECTIONS AND EXERCISES

1. The assumption of scarcity. Gandhi said, "Live simply so that others might simply live. Parker Palmer, adds to this saying, "Our souls and the lives of others hang in the balance." If you mostly live out of an assumption of scarcity, what might you see and change in order to live more fully out of an assumption of abundance?

2. Grasping and letting go. And He said to them, "Take care! Be on your guard against all kinds of greed for one's life does not consist in the abundance of possessions" (Luke 12:15). Abundance comes not from possessing, but from sharing what seems scarce in our life. Grasping for more brings less, whereas letting go brings forth more. In what ways are you grasping for more than your share or sharing what seems scarce in your life? What would help you see today, your life, as blessing?

REFLECTION 15: GRATITUDE

What good is it for someone to gain the whole world, yet forfeit their soul?
Mark 8:36

THANK GOD AND PAY IT FORWARD

As Beth and I sat vigil during her sister's final hours, we opened her bible looking for comfort. We found scribbled on a piece of paper Norma's own prayer: *"Is there anything I would hold onto, rather than let God use it, for the building of the Reign of God, or to the greater honor and glory of God? My own will? Self-determination? My right to choose?"* These were not the words of a woman dying of cancer trying to bargain for more time. These were the words of a woman who lived her entire life with gratitude. This was a woman whose faith started and ended with gratitude – simple, grace-filled gratitude.

Contrast Norma with our neighbor, Tom, who lived across the street from us. Tom had invented a grease trap and made millions. I'm ashamed to admit it, but I sometimes feel envious of people, like Tom, who seem to have it all handed to them on a silver platter. He seemed to have not a care in the world and, by all worldly measures of success, had "made it" by age 32. By age 35, he had drunk himself to death. His life had become consumed with the material goods he had amassed and the ones he was still chasing. He had it all but had lost his soul. He was, at the end of his life, ungrateful, emotionally destitute and spiritually impoverished.

Tom's story seems to validate what Jesus said, that it is more difficult for the rich to enter the kingdom of heaven than it is for a camel to pass through the eye of a needle (Mark 10:25). I don't believe it is because God loves a person who is poor more than one who is rich. But it makes sense that the poor are more predisposed to God's love. They have not been indoctrinated into the unnatural state of ingratitude or lured away from genuine love by its material substitutes. They literally can't afford to be consumed by material things.

The average American watches 5 hours of television per day, 25% of which is advertisements. Over a lifetime, we can expect to sit through 3 solid years of advertising. We are indoctrinated into believing that we do not have enough. The system depends on it. We are conditioned into a state of ingratitude for what we possess or embarrassment for who we have become. It's not natural. We didn't start out this way as kids. We didn't have this chronic sense of dissatisfaction or envy by comparing ourselves to what others have.

We are as captive as those to whom Jeremiah spoke, "This is what the Lord says: 'What fault did your ancestors find in me, that they strayed so far from me? They followed worthless idols and became worthless themselves.'" (Jeremiah. 2:5). Gratitude is simple and natural. We have only to look at what we do have, rather than what we don't. We have only to look at who we are, rather than who we are not. We have only to recognize that, by the grace of God, we have received the gift of life. The inner work of transformation invites you to explore your basis for gratitude and the false idols that potentially hold you captive.

MEDITATIONS

Mary Jo Leddy. Radical Gratitude

Radical gratitude begins when we stop taking life for granted. It arises in the astonishment at the miracle of creation and of our own creation.... In gratitude, the vicious cycle of dissatisfaction with life is broken and we begin anew in the recognition of what we have rather than in what we don't, in the acknowledgement of who we are rather than in the awareness of who we aren't. Gratitude is the foundation of faith in God as the Creator of all beginnings, great and small. It awakens the imagination to another way of being, to another kind of economy, the great economy of grace in which each person is of infinite value and worth.

Hafiz

Even after all this time, the sun never says to the earth: "You owe me." Look what happens with a love like that. It lights up the whole sky.

Psalms 118:24

This is the day which the LORD has made; Let us rejoice and be glad in it.

1 Corinthians 15:10

But by the grace of God I am what I am, and his grace toward me was not in vain. On the contrary, I worked harder than any of them, though it was not I, but the grace of God that is with me.

Nan C. Merrill. Psalms for Praying: An Invitation to Wholeness

I give You thanks, O Blessed One, with my whole heart; before all the people I sing your praise; I was humbled when I came to see that you dwell in me, in the Holy Temple of all souls; my gratitude knows no bounds.

JOURNAL REFLECTIONS AND EXERCISES

1. What prevents you from experiencing more gratitude in your life?

2. Pay it forward. We can be grateful for what we have been given, but giving can also move us to gratitude. One of the best antidotes to feeling ungrateful for what we don't have is to give to someone more in need. Give something to someone in need in the next few days and reflect on the experience. Pay it forward and see what that does for you.

3. Giving thanks. Take some time to reflect upon who and what has helped you to become the person you are with all that you have in life. For whom, and for what, do you feel the most grateful in your life? Give thanks where thanks is due and find a way to express your gratitude.

4. Express your gratitude. Reflect upon who is in your life that you might be taking for granted. Sometimes you wait until it's too late to let them know what they mean to you. Write this person a letter expressing your gratitude and share this with them. Or bring them a gift for no other reason than to say "thanks."

PART VI:
WRITING A
NEW NARRATIVE

You need only claim the events of your life to make yourself yours. When you truly possess all you have been and done... you are fierce with reality.
Florida Scott Maxwell

THE STORIES THAT SHAPE OUR LIVES

Stories have immense power to shape our identities and our destiny. Naturally, we make meaning of the events and experiences of our lives by how we filter, interpret and make connections. Myth or fact, these strands of interpreted events are woven into stories we tell others and ourselves about our lives. Over time, these stories become self-reinforcing, often referred to as "confirmation bias." We filter new events as validation for the stories we have already formed, and we filter out the ones that don't fit. Our narratives shape our filters and our choices, form our values, determine how we understand life, and solidify our identity and determine our destiny.

Some narratives we construct about our lives are empowering and help us grow. They bring out the best of who we are, build on grace and liberate our spirit. Other narratives born of shame are falsely constructed, outdated or disempowering. They keep us from growing, engender poor self-esteem and undermine our best intentions. These feed on regret, guilt and shame. They evoke feelings of unworthiness, inadequacy and self-condemnation.

The inner work of writing a new narrative calls us to become aware of the stories we have constructed and rewrite these in ways that conform with reality, offer us hope and engender meaning and purpose. This inner work involves reinforcing those narratives that are empowering, while reframing the ones that are disempowering. This is an opportunity to look at our life through new eyes, with more wisdom than we had when we were younger.

Writing a new narrative is more than just finding the silver lining or making lemonade out of lemons. Rather, this is the work of listening to our soul's understanding of the meaning of our experience and discerning how we can use our understanding to facilitate growth. It is about becoming conscious of the inner voices that sap our energy, dim our vision and sabotage our attempts to grow. It is the profound, spiritual work of listening to the deep story within us that is continually seeking to unfold throughout our lives.

Your inner work invites you to look at your life through the lens of your higher consciousness in order to facilitate your soul's journey toward growth.

REFLECTION 16: NEW BEGINNINGS

Who made the world? Who made the swan, and the black bear? Who made the grasshopper? This grasshopper, I mean, the one who has flung herself out of the grass, the one who is eating sugar out of my hand, who is moving her jaws back and forth instead of up and down, who is gazing around with her enormous and complicated eyes. Now she lifts her pale forearms and thoroughly washes her face. Now she snaps her wings open, and floats away. I don't know exactly what a prayer is. I do know how to pay attention, how to fall down into the grass, how to kneel down in the grass, how to be idle and blessed, how to stroll through the fields, which is what I have been doing all day. Tell me, what else should I have done? Doesn't everything die at last, and too soon? Tell me, what is it you plan to do with your one, wild and precious life?
Mary Oliver. The Summer Day

BIRTHING A NEW WAY OF BEING: FROM LEGACY TO NEW LIFE

Simply put, a legacy is how we will be remembered and the mark we have had upon our world. Our legacy does not end with retirement from our productive years. Nor does it even end when we die. It lives on in the lives of those we've touched during our lifetime, far beyond what we can ever anticipate or know. What will you do with your one, wild and precious life? What will you do, just for the love of it with the time you have left?

Thus far, you have done a great deal of inner work to let go and make room for new life. The inner work of transformation also includes a birthing of new life for our world, for your community and for your own personal future. However, the future is not in some distant time or place; the future is here and now. Now, what is emerging in your heart? Now, what are your hopes and dreams? Let your life speak, listen to your urgent longings, and set your sights upon the horizon.

Howard Thurman, a theologian and civil rights leader, once said, "Don't ask what the world needs. Ask what makes you come alive and go out and do it. Because what the world needs is people who have come alive." Our soul comes alive at the intersection of our heart's desires and the needs of our wounded world. This is not as hard to discover as it is to go out and do. It is the doing that makes the difference.

In their book, *Active Hope*, Janna Macy and Chris Johnstone draw the distinction between the kind of hope that speaks of our preferred future and the kind of hope that speaks to our desire. The former is about "hopefulness" and the latter is about "active hope." This means that you will take steps now to bring to fruition what you love and want to see happen. What do you hope your future will be and how will you cooperate with grace to see that it happens?

MEDITATIONS

Richard Lewis. Living By Wonder

In our grasshopper and salamander days, who among us didn't ask why the grasshopper could jump so far – or why the salamander had black dots on its orange body? We trampled leaves with our feet just to hear what kind of sounds leaves made. We threw flat stones over the surface of streams to see how far the stones could skip. We listened to crickets cry in nights far beyond our grasp of what the darkness was. We slept, only to wake, with the strange sense of how could we be awake when we had only just been sleeping.

In those days, we knew as much as we had to know in order to ask what we didn't know. Our ignorance wasn't just innocence, but the foundation from which we offered ourselves the daily surprise of discovering another question, another way to uncover something mysterious, something we hadn't understood yesterday. We lived by wonder for, by wondering, we were able to multiply a growing consciousness of being alive.

Richard Rohr. Things Hidden

Spiritually speaking, it does not help to give people quick conclusions before they have made any inner journeys. They will always misunderstand them or misuse them, and it will separate them from astonishment.

Luke 13:18-19

Then Jesus asked, "What is the kingdom of God like? What shall I compare it to? It is like a mustard seed, which a man took and planted in his garden. It grew and became a tree, and the birds perched in its branches."

Luke 17:20-21

Being asked by the Pharisees when the kingdom of God would come, he answered them, "The kingdom of God is not coming in ways that can be observed, nor will they say, 'Look, here it is!' or 'There!' for behold, the kingdom of God is in the midst of you."

Albert Camus

In the midst of winter, I finally learned that there is, in me, an invincible summer.

Francis Thompson. The Hound of Heaven

Alack, thou knowest not
How little worthy of any love thou art!
Whom wilt thou find to love ignoble thee,
Save Me, save only Me?
All which I took from thee
I did but take,
Not for thy harms,
But that thou might'st seek it in My arms.
All which thy child's mistake
Fancies as lost, I have stored for thee at home:
Rise, clasp my hand and come!

JOURNAL REFLECTIONS AND EXERCISES

Living in the middle time

Living in the middle time, betwixt and between what was and what is yet to be, is a challenge for everyone. It was a challenge for St. John of the Cross, Oscar Romero, and all those who enter the dark night of the soul. This is a liminal time (dark night, desert, wilderness, or whatever name you give it), a time of confusion, ambiguity, tension, mourning, laboring, birthing and all the pain and ecstasy that is intrinsic in the lived *experience* of transformation. Most people, unable to withstand the tumultuous experience of a middle-time, will rush to pre-mature closure and, thereby, abort its transformative potential.

1.   However long the night. Nancy Schreck, in her 2014 keynote address at LCWR, implored those present "to be faithful, however long the night."

   a.   What do you need to do in order to be faithful, however long the night? Identify three specific actions.

b. How might you live well and stay nourished amidst the ambiguity, tension, grieving, laboring and birthing that must be done during this liminal time? Identify three specific behavioral choices you could make.

c. What will help you stay in the struggle and keep you from aborting this work when the going gets tough? Identify three specific action steps.

2. What do you hope your future will be, and how will you cooperate with grace to see that it happens? Commit yourself to five intentions for the next five years. A commitment is something you *will* do, not something you will *try* to do or *wish* to do. This is not about a large bucket list or indulging in fantasy. This is about goals you are committed to achieve within the next five years. They need to be rooted in your soul's energy and passions.

As such, this exercise involves reflecting upon your inner life, taking into account your wisdom, gifts, and what brings you joy, as well as reflecting upon your desired service to your community and to the world. Write and rewrite these until you have them right. Envision having accomplished each one. Feel what you imagine you will feel when you reach your goals. Write it, paint it, make poetry of it; do whatever it takes to help you know this deep within your soul, as this will become your active hope for the future.

Now declare it! What five things will you do, or become, in the next five years that bespeak your longings, your wonders or your loves? Describe each of these commitments in one sentence. Then place your words (symbols or artwork) on a mantle, by your nightstand, in your sacred space, somewhere, as a daily reminder of your commitments.

Reflection 17:
Let Your Life Speak

Before you tell your life what you intend to do with it, listen for what it intends to do with you. Before you tell your life what truths and values you have decided to live up to, let your life tell you what truths you embody, what values you represent.
Parker Palmer. Let Your Life Speak

Who are you growing to become?

The Quakers have a belief about truth and enlightenment. They tell us "Let your life speak" to suggest that our life as we have lived it offers us intimations as to our authentic values and our God-given purpose for living. Parker Palmer suggests that it is more important to listen to our life's ever unfolding efforts to actualize our own true nature than it is to embrace a long list of ideals, however noble or virtuous. Our life's journey gives us clues, he suggests, to our true vocation. The path that God intends for us, in other words, does not come from our own willfulness. It is not a goal to pursue; rather, it is discerned through our listening. Before I can tell my life what I want to do with it, I must listen to my life telling me who I am.

164

Gandhi speaks of our life's journey as a "great experiment" with the truth. Palmer adds to this by saying, "True self, when violated, will always resist us, sometimes at great cost, holding our lives in check until we honor its truth." Rosa Parks knew this, Martin Luther King knew this. All of us, at some level, realize this: we cannot act outwardly in a way that contradicts our inner truth without paying a great price.

The poet Rumi also knew this, and he links the personal and communal costs together: "If you are here unfaithfully with us, you're causing terrible damage," he says. "We will make promises we cannot keep, build houses from flimsy stuff, conjure dreams that devolve into nightmares, and other people will suffer – if we are unfaithful to our true self."

How many times in life have we come to know this from our own experience? When unaware of our limitations, our vulnerability or our own sinfulness, we must eventually come to own it and reckon with our own humanness, or we pay a terrible price. When we have renounced the gifts and abundant blessings we have received in our life, our task is to reclaim these, as well. We must play the hand we are dealt with circumstances that are ours, embracing the truth of who we are being called to become, and trust that we, in our embracing of this call, are surely more than enough.

The inner work of transformation invites you to let your life speak, to reflect upon the unfolding journey of your life and to glean from these reflections who you are growing to become. You are invited to reflect upon the shifts that have occurred over the years in your life, the challenges that are before you and the horizon opportunities ahead. As you listen to what your life has to say to you, ask yourself, *Is the life I am living the life that wants to live in me? Ask yourself, What does my life intend for me? Who am I growing to become?*

Parker Palmer says, "The world still waits for the truth that will set us free – my truth, your truth, our truth – the truth that was seeded in the earth when each of us arrived here formed in the image of God. Cultivating that truth, I believe, is the authentic vocation of every human being." Jesus says, "You will know the Truth, and the Truth will set you free" (John 8:32). Listen to the truth that your soul intends by reflecting upon your own life journey.

MEDITATIONS

Terry Tempest Williams. Red: Passion and Patience in the Desert

The eyes of the future are looking back at us and they are praying for us to see beyond our own time. They are kneeling with hands clasped that we might act with restraint, that we might leave room for the life that is destined to come. To protect what is wild is to protect what is gentle. Perhaps the wildness we fear is the pause between our own heartbeats, the silent space that says we live only by grace. Wilderness lives by this same grace. Wild mercy is in our hands.

Romans 8:19

All creation is eagerly expecting the transformation of the People of God.

Mark 8:27-29

Jesus went on with his disciples to the villages of Caesarea Philippi; and on the way he asked his disciples, "Who do people say that I am?" And they answered him, "John the Baptist; and others Elijah; and still others, one of the prophets." He asked them, "But who do you say that I am?" Peter answered, "You are the Messiah."

Joan Chittister. Between the Dark and the Daylight

The lifelong question now became what was worse – having to face the long-term sting of shame or bear the short-term pain of truth. And so began my journey from guilt to growth. It became what the Church calls, in its explanation of sin as the reason for the coming of Jesus, "the happy fault." The understanding of sin that comes from careless sinning itself, the necessary fault that turns our life around, that becomes a wisdom to live by. As I have listened to people over the years, I have become more and more convinced that everyone deals, sometime in life, with a necessary fault. What's more I am convinced that most people need the Rubicon of the necessary fault. We must consciously begin to choose the kind of person we want to be in life.

JOURNAL REFLECTIONS AND EXERCISES

1. Life changes. As you reflect upon your life from young adulthood until now, what growth and changes have you seen in your:

    a. Spiritual life (i.e., prayer and contemplative practices; language and style; common prayer and individual prayer), and what impact has this made upon your life?

    b. Ministry endeavors (e.g., type, choices, effectiveness) and what impact has this had upon your life?

    c. Community life (e.g., ways of living in community and relating to others) and what difference has this made in your life?

    d. Stewardship practices (e.g., personal, spiritual, material and financial) and what difference has this made in your life?

2. Becoming. In light of your evolving journey, what do you see as horizon opportunities in your life (i.e., areas of challenge or growth potential) that give you hope and passion? In other words, who do you see yourself growing to become?

Reflection 18:
Back to the Future

The future influences the present just as much as the past.
Friedrich Nietzsche

Looking back from the future

Granted, it is impossible to know what the future holds, particularly in times of transition. The future is unpredictable and unpicturable. Still, if we are not to just let the future happen to us, if we are to be proactive agents in shaping our own future, we have to make decisions based upon what we hope the future will be. One of the most challenging aspects of this effort is the ability to imagine. We need to use our imagination to think beyond what we already see and know in the present. And we need to tie our imagination to our hope, our longings, for new life.

When we look upon a field that we have seen daily, it is nearly impossible to see the new green shoots of grass emerging amid the grass that was there yesterday. But new seeds of life and new green shoots are there. We see what we are used to seeing. We are, in a sense, blinded in seeing the new life because we project into it the life we have seen all along. We see what we expect to see.

Time projection helps us see the possibilities of the "new" by moving our mental fences out into the future. Time projection is a technique used by psychologists and hypnotherapists to stir a person's imagination and help them get beyond what they know and have already experienced in order to discover new possibilities. It helps people get beyond stewing in their juices, seeing what they have always seen, and open the door to new possibilities.

Deepak Chopra tell us: "Our minds influence the key activity of the brain, which then influences everything; perception, cognition, thoughts and feelings, personal relationships; they're all a projection of you." Time projection is a projection of you. It is not a way to picture the unpicturable, not a test of your clairvoyant abilities, but it is a way to unearth what is in your imagination. It is a way to open up possibilities and project into them your hopes, dreams and yearning for new life. For you to give birth to new life, to bring forth new life, you first need to stir your imagination with the elixir of hope.

MEDITATIONS

John Surette

We cannot go into the future without our past, our tradition, but these cannot lead us there. We need to look beyond the past and not hold on too tightly to our tradition. What leads us into the future are our imaginations, our creativities, our dreams, our vision, and our allurements. We are not so much people of the past as we are people of the future. We are people of the newness that has been promised and the newness that we are bringing about through our efforts as co-creators. 'See I am doing something new! Do you not perceive it?'

Jeremiah 29:11

"For I know the plans I have for you," declares the Lord, "plans to prosper you and not harm you, plans to give you hope and a future."

Proverbs 29:18

"Where there is no vision, the people perish."

Charles Kettering

Our imagination is the only limit to what we can hope to have in the future.

Steven Spielberg. Back to the future

When Marty claims to be from 1985, 1955 Doc asks him, "Tell me, Future Boy, who's President of the United States in 1985?" Marty says, "Ronald Reagan," and Doc laughs, "Ronald Reagan? The actor? Ha! Then who's Vice President, Jerry Lewis? I suppose Jane Wyman is the First Lady. And Jack Benny is Secretary of the Treasury!"

JOURNAL REFLECTIONS AND EXERCISES

Write a letter: Back To The Future

As you journey more deeply into shaping your future, I am asking you to prepare a *letter*. This letter is then to be shared with others in your small group or larger faith community. This will not only stir your hopes and imagination for the future, but it will do the same for those with whom you share it. It can provide food for the journey.

I hope that you will consider this letter as one of the most important letters you will ever write, that the shaping of your very future depends on it. I ask that you take this invitation into prayer and let it ripen, pouring new wine into new wineskins, until you are sure of what you want to say. Take it down into the depths of your soul and speak of your deepest longings for your own future and the future of your community.

What am I asking you to write? I want build upon what you have thus far reflected upon and shared with your small group. Where do you imagine you are being led personally and as a faith community? Having listened to the dreams of the future from some of our sisters and associates, what are your dreams for the future?

I want you to walk with one of your cherished ancestors in prayer and talk with him or her about the future of your community. Choose a spiritual companion who has been dearest in your heart and with whom you could have an imaginary, prayerful, soul-to-soul conversation. It might be a Saint, your community's founder, or Jesus. It might be a wisdom figure in your community or a mentor of some kind. Choose someone who knows you, knows your life and who you know, deep inside, would only want what is good and right for you, your community and those you serve.

For example, if you chose to pray and talk with Jesus, ask what he sees in your future. What are his deepest longings for you? What might you look like five years from now if you look through his eyes? What does he see happening? What might be your community's mission in the future if you are listening to his deepest desires for you? How might you be living community five years from now? How might the spirit of your charism come alive in today's world? In his heart-of-hearts, how does he hope you and your community will be transformed? Pray with Jesus on the road to Emmaus. Walk with your ancestors and dream of the possibilities.

Once you've had time to let your dream ripen, write a letter to your faith community as if you are writing it 5 years hence, looking back from the future on all that has happened. Project in your imagination all that has emerged in the last five years and what your life might be like at that point.

Write to your members as if you are the voice of the one with whom you chose to pray (i.e., your spiritual companion). Or, if you prefer, use your own voice having taken to heart what your spiritual companion shared with you. Write from the depths of your soul a very personal letter that speaks of your deepest longings. Write to your members telling them what you see as the future of your community five years from now. Write it out of unwavering faith, audacious hope and most especially with love for your members, companions in mission and a wounded world in need of your charism.

Reflection 19:
Urgent Longings

Grace happens when we explore the deep inner currents of belonging and realize the profound connection between our aspirations for life and the concrete requirements for living.
James Conlon

Whispers of grace

James Conlon wrote, "Grace happens when, in the midst of our search, we discover that place of hope where our secret longings lie." When I first read his words, I wondered to myself: *What is a longing and how is it different from a need or a want?* I know I want to fly again as this was a passion I begrudgingly relinquished several years back. My wings have been clipped and I no longer fly. I would like to play a game of golf and someday score par. I need to lose those pesky fifteen pounds to get to my "ideal weight." Oh, well. As I listen to these personal passions, wants and needs, they don't strike me as longings.

My oldest daughter, Kelly, served as a nurse in Baghdad. In reflecting about my longings, I discovered that I long for her soul to be forever healed from the ravages of war. I have a longing for my prodigal son, Jeff, that his soul will continue healing from wounds he carries as a result of his parents' divorce. I have a longing for my youngest daughter, Colleen, to discover her own inner wisdom and spiritual path. I long for my wife, Beth and I to live a life of leisure with the same passion and priority that we have given our ministry for so many years. Such longings, I thought, go beyond wants and needs, and bring me to the soulwork of my life.

Judy Schroeder, who says: "Deep within the heart there is a primal pain of longing, the cry of the soul separated from its source. The pain comes from the memory of when we were together with God. This process allows us special moments in our life when we can taste of this union, a taste of the divine remembrance." The primal pain of longing seems to only increase with time. The taste of divine remembrance grows sweeter. Can you taste it?

Thomas Merton wrote: "If I never become what I am meant to be, but always remain what I am not, I shall spend eternity contradicting myself by being, at once, something and nothing, a life that wants to live and is dead and a death that wants to be dead and cannot quite achieve its own death because it still has to exist." These words, for me, strike a deep cord of knowing that our soul is forever calling us home to places that are both familiar and forever mysterious. Who we are always holds the tension between who we have been and who we are growing to become.

For those on a faith journey, this paradoxical tension invites us to reckon with our hidden payoffs for denying our own goodness. This is where our loyalties to the way things have always been come face-to-face with our fidelity to the truths we are growing to discover, along with the current realities that insist upon new wineskins. This is where our growing edges encroach upon the status quo of relationships, causing us to look anew at what we have hidden from one another, kept from the people we love, and stashed under a bushel basket. This tension is our soul's longing to let go, reconcile, and rebirth.

MEDITATIONS

Rainer Maria Rilke

God speaks to each of us as he makes us, then walks with us silently out of the night. These are the words we dimly hear: You, sent out beyond your recall, go to the limits of your longing. Embody me. Flare up like flame and make big shadows I can move in. Let everything happen to you: beauty and terror. Just keep going. No feeling is final. Don't let yourself lose me. Nearby is the country they call life. You will know it by its seriousness. Give me your hand.

Jeremiah 29:10-14

For thus says the Lord: When seventy years are completed for Babylon, I will visit you, and I will fulfill to you my promise and bring you back to this place. For I know the plans I have for you, declares the Lord, plans for welfare and not for evil, to give you a future full of hope. Then you will call upon me and come and pray to me, and I will hear you. You will seek me and find me, when you seek me with all your heart. I will be found by you, declares the Lord, and I will restore your fortunes and gather you from all the nations and all the places where I have driven you, declares the Lord, and I will bring you back to the place from which I sent you into exile.

Anne Quigley. There Is A Longing

There is a longing in our hearts, O Lord, for you to reveal yourself to us.
There is a longing in our hearts for love we only find in you, our God.
For justice, for freedom, for mercy: hear our prayer.
In sorrow, in grief: be near, hear our prayer, O God.
There is a longing in our hearts, O Lord, for you to reveal yourself to us.
There is a longing in our hearts for love we only find in you, our God.
For wisdom, for courage, for comfort: hear our prayer.
In weakness, in fear: be near, hear our prayer, O God.
There is a longing in our hearts, O Lord, for you to reveal yourself to us.
There is a longing in our hearts for love we only find in you, our God.
For healing, for wholeness, for new life: hear our prayer.

In sickness, in death: be near, hear our prayer, O God.
There is a longing in our hearts, O Lord, for you to reveal yourself to us.
There is a longing in our hearts for love we only find in you, our God.
Lord, save us, take pity, light in our darkness.
We call you, we wait: be near, hear our prayer, O God.
There is a longing in our hearts, O Lord, for you to reveal yourself to us.
There is a longing in our hearts for love we only find in you, our God.

Journal Reflections and Exercises

1. Longing. As you reflect upon your life today, and reach deeply into your heart and soul, what are your urgent longings? Distinguish these from needs and wants. Let the question sink into your soul. Reflect and write without judgment. Let the words spill out of you and fall onto the paper.

2. Goodness meant to live. What goodness within yourself have you hidden in a bushel basket and kept from the people you love? What would it be like for you to bring this goodness more fully into your life?

REFLECTION 20: FLOURISHING

Flourishing goes beyond happiness, or satisfaction with life. True, people who are flourishing are happy. But that's not the half of it. Beyond feeling good, they are also doing good, adding value to the world.
Barbara Fredrickson

LIVING IN THE PRESENT

In recent years, my wife and I have made it a practice to go to Kauai in the winter to rejuvenate our souls, a kind of sabbath. Part of that rejuvenation is the time we spend with a woman we've befriended. Renee lives completely on providence, has no possessions other than what's in her ancient Subaru, and she is engaged entirely with the flow of life. Approaching 70, she swims each morning with the whales, gives massages (while offering spiritual advice) to the tourists during the day, and climbs the Napoli coast on the weekends (in her bare feet, no less). She is the Spirit of Kauai, the living embodiment of Aloha, living in the flow and fullness of life. It's a soul-shifting experience for me when I'm with her. How is that Renee can flourish with seemingly so few possessions in her life, relying entirely on the universe for everything?

In his book, *Flourish*, Martin Seligman explains that Aristotle's belief that human action is singularly motivated by happiness is a misnomer. To flourish, he says, is our life's motivation. And he offers five key elements that result in the experience of flourishing:

1. **Positive emotion.** When my 101-year-old stepfather recently stopped playing golf, I asked him, "Frank, why did you stop playing?" He thought for a moment and said, "Ted, the joy just went out of it." If there is no joy in our life we are not flourishing. We are languishing.

2. **Achievement.** This does not mean you have to climb Mount Everest or become master chef. It is achievement for its own sake. A goal might be as small as taking a walk, finishing the laundry, or spending some time with a friend. It doesn't matter how large or small the goals are, just that you have them. Life takes on meaning when you become motivated, set goals every day and charge after them.

3. **Positive relationships.** Spend time with people whose company you enjoy. These are people whose company you love because they make you laugh, they build you up, they give you energy. They do not put you down or drag you down.

4. **Engagement.** Engagement is about presence or being in the flow of life. You are in the flow if you are so absorbed with something or someone that you lose track of time. You don't have to be a jazz musician to do this. Being in the flow means being present, living in the present, engaging in whatever life dishes up.

5. **Meaning.** This is not about some large philosophical definition of meaning, but serving some purpose larger than our own ego, seeing our self as part of a larger world or universe.

These five elements, says Seligman, enable us to flourish in life. They enable us to embrace the abundance that life has to offer. The first four of these are fairly self-explanatory, so let me share a bit on meaning because it is a bit harder to grasp.

I have often said to communities, "When a community has more memories than dreams, it is dying." I think the same thing is true for individuals. We need to dream. We need to have goals – something to live for. We all know people whose spirits died before their bodies. And we all know people who lived well beyond what their terminal diagnosis warranted for no other reason than their tenacious will to live. We need to live a life with meaning and purpose or we begin to wither and die. Meaning, according to Viktor Frankl, is a "fundamental lifeforce" that nourishes and vivifies the soul.

John Milton once said, "The mind is its own place, and in itself can make a heaven of hell" or "a hell of heaven." Frankl understood this. He shared his experience of living in the most hellish circumstances imaginable, the death camps of WWII, while finding a place of meaning and purpose. He observed and wrote of a helpful distinction between those prisoners who lived a provisional existence versus those who lived with meaning and purpose.

Those who lived a provisional existence were those he described as lifeless, the ones who walked like ghosts in a fog-like state. They numbed their pain by dissociating themselves from their present reality. They literally stopped being present, stopped living in the present and, consequently, stopped making choices from within their present realities to transform their suffering. They lost their will to live and, in so doing, they hastened their own death.

The ones who survived lived in the same hellacious circumstances, yet found meaning and purpose where they could, even if only on the smallest scale. They seized upon opportunities to find beauty in a sunset, kindness in sharing a piece of bread, mercy toward another's suffering, joy in another's smile. They lived in the present and made choices that transformed their pain into compassion, mercy, kindness, joy, beauty or love. In Frankl's words: "Everything can be taken from us but one thing: the last of the human freedoms…, to choose one's attitude in any given set of circumstances, to choose one's own way."

Flourishing begins with a choice. "Every moment of one's existence, said Norman Mailer, "one is growing into more or retreating into less." We can choose, in other words, to be a plaything of circumstances, feeling hapless, hopeless and helpless; or we can accept the hand we've been dealt, listen for a deeper invitation, and make choices that preserve our freedom. We can listen to that still small voice urging us to "choose life."

Engage the flow of life, become immersed, even if only for a short time, in a game, a meaningful conversation, some kind of personal challenge to stretch your skills and learn something new. Instead of checking your phone 72 times per day, set some boundaries and check your text or email only a few times per day. Clear out the clutter of distractions. Let these small wins remind you of the kind of energy and enthusiasm you've been missing. We need to give meaning to life, not wait for life to give us meaning.

MEDITATIONS

Genesis 26:22

He moved on from there and dug another well, and no one quarreled over it. He named it Rehoboth, saying, "Now the Lord has given us room and we will flourish in the land."

Numbers 13:27

And they told him, "We came to the land to which you sent us. It flows with milk and honey, and this is its fruit."

Viktor Frankl

Everything can be taken from man but one thing: the last of the human freedoms – to choose one's attitude in any given set of circumstances, to choose one's own way.

Derek Rydall

As we emerge into our full potential and activate our deepest purpose, the gifts we share create and support an ecosystem that allows our world to evolve and thrive.

Joseph Campbell

Everything is conspiring for your good, awakening your deeper potential, and preparing you for greater things, whether it's meant to land you on the front page of the paper or the front porch of a neighbor in need. But to harvest the blessings of your journey, you must practice this awareness, reinterpreting everything you see until you see the divine conspiracy everywhere.

Ted Dunn

See video: Flourishing in a season of surrender. (https://vimeo.com/548935579)

JOURNAL REFLECTIONS AND EXERCISES

We can flourish in any season of life, from toddlerhood to elderhood. It is about having joy, being with people we love, being present and living in the present, and creating a life with meaning and purpose. Even in the most difficult of circumstance, we have choices, the freedom to choose and a chance to change. We can make choices that leave us to languish or choices that help us flourish.

1. What does it mean for you to flourish in this season of life?

2. What choices are your making:

   a. What brings you joy?

   b. In whose company do you come alive?

   c. What are your goals, large or small, and how are you charging after them?

   d. When do you find yourself totally present, in the present, living in the flow of life?

   e. What gives meaning to your life?

*I said to my soul, be still and wait without hope, for hope
would be hope for the wrong thing; wait without love, for
love would be love of the wrong thing; there is yet faith, but
the faith and the love are all in the waiting. Wait without
thought, for you are not ready for thought: So the darkness
shall be the light, and the stillness the dancing.*
T.S. Eliot

About The Author

Dr. Ted Dunn is a clinical psychologist and co-founder of Comprehensive Consulting Services, Clearwater, FL. He has experience as a consultant, facilitator, professor, psychotherapist, and supervisor to professionals in the field of mental health. He obtained his undergraduate training at Ohio State University, and his Master's and Doctoral degrees in Clinical Psychology from St. Louis University. He completed his graduate training in 1985 following his internship at Rutgers Medical School in New Jersey where he concentrated on psychodynamic psychotherapy and systems interventions.

He has advanced training in psychoanalytic psychotherapy from the St. Louis Psychoanalytic Institute as well as family therapy and systems applications from masters in the field (e.g., Jay Haley, Salvador Minuchin, Virginia Satir and Monica McGoldrick). He has extensive experience with psychological assessment methods and has consulted, taught, published, developed labs for hospitals, and served as an expert witness in these fields.

As an outgrowth of his clinical experience, Dr. Dunn's practice has evolved and today focuses upon consultation, training and facilitation services provided to Catholic religious communities and other faith-based organizations throughout the United States and internationally. He has been working with religious men and women since the 1980's and sees his training and experience as particularly suited for this population.

He has written extensively about Religious Life and regularly facilitates and presents at Chapters and assemblies. He consults with leadership teams and assists communities in planning, visioning, and communal discernment. His current focus is on guiding communities who are discerning God's call to new life through processes of deep change and transformation. His recent book (*Graced Crossroads*), along with this companion book (*The Inner Work of Transformation*) demonstrate his capacity to integrate spirituality, psychology and systems theory.

The integration of spirituality, psychology and value-based skills are key to his efforts. Though the approaches and populations he has served have varied over the years, his *compassionate approach to healing, belief in the natural resiliency of the human spirit, and personal commitment to life-long learning* remain the foundation to all his professional endeavors. These are the bedrock to his current call to minister to faith-based organizations, empowering them to live well and mutually partner in creating a future.

Notes

i. Ted Dunn, *Graced Crossroads: Pathways to Deep Change and Transformation*, First ed. (St. Charles, MO: CCS Publications, 2020).

ii. Ibid., p.194.

iii. Robert E. Quinn, *Deep Change: Discovering the Leader Within*, Jossey-Bass Business & Management Series (San Francisco, Calif.: Jossey-Bass Publishers, 1996), p.3.

iv. David J. Nygren and Miriam D. Ukeritis, *The Future of Religious Orders in the United States: Transformation and Commitment* (Westport, Conn.: Praeger, 1993), p.259.

v. Edward Teller, Goodreads, Inc., https://www.goodreads.com/quotes/69423-when-you-come-to-the-end-of-all-the-light.

vi. Thomas Merton, *Thoughts in Solitude* (New York,: Farrar, 1958), p.83.

vii. Marcia Allen, "Transformation – an Experiment in Hope," in *Leadership Conference of Religious Women* (Orlando,2016), p.5-7.

viii. Ken Untener, "A Future Not Our Own: In Memory of Oscar Romero (1917–1980)," *The mystery of the Romero Prayer* (1979), https://www.journeywithjesus.net/PoemsAndPrayers/Ken_Unten-er_A_Future_Not_Our_Own.shtml.

[ix] Václav Havel and Karel Hvížďala, *Disturbing the Peace : A Conversation with Karel HvíŽĎAla*, 1st American ed. (New York: Knopf : Distributed by Random House, 1990), p.181.

[x] Joan Chittister, *Scarred by Struggle, Transformed by Hope* (Grand Rapids, Mich.: William B. Eerdmans Pub.: Ottawa Novalis, Saint Paul University, 2003), p.2.

[xi] Ibid., p.19.

[xii] Joanna Macy and Chris Johnstone, *Active Hope : How to Face the Mess We're in without Going Crazy* (Novato, Calif.: New World Library, 2012).

[xiii] Tina Turner, "What's Love Got to Do with It," in *What's Love Got to Do with It* (Parlophone, 1993).

[xiv] Richard Rohr, *The Naked Now: Learning to See as the Mystics See* (New York: Crossroad Pub. Co., 2009), p.122.

[xv] Jean Pierre Medaille, *Maxims of the Little Institute*, Writings of Jean Pierre Medaille, Maxim 84 (Toronto, CA: Sisters of St. Joseph of Toronto, 1985), p.139.